MY MANY QUESTIONS TO GOD

By
Michelle Jean

MY MANY QUESTIONS TO GOD

Good God as you make a true way for me I truly thank you because I need you; will always need you.

You are my way and as I walk through your open door please take my hand and hold on to me.

Wrap your gentle and powerful arms around me and smile down at me and say Michelle, thank you I truly love you more than unconditionally.

You are my good choice and I am sorry for all the trials and tribulations you face but you had to for my sake.

You had to because you've proven to me and all that one did love me truthfully more than unconditionally.

You showed me what true love is and despite our battles you were always fair and just.

You are strong willed and you are true love and I truly love you more than so.

Ah Lovey, I cherish you and look forward to the day when I can speak with you face to face.

Pain and loneliness is there Good God, so no more trials and tribulations for me and my family including the good and true seeds you've given me.

MY MANY QUESTIONS TO GOD

Good God give us the victory over our enemies. The earth is full of evil Lovey and this should not be. Hence I am asking you to make a way for us and our people.

Good God wicked and evil people dominate and control and I need this to stop Lovey.

I need good and true peace, homes and clean living here on earth.

My Darling, bathe me today from head to toe. Dry my hair and braid it for me. I need to be clean because I do not feel clean.

My Darling, bathe me and make me clean because my job is not done with you. So truly stand beside me and let's make right the wrongs done to you by man – humans and spirit.

My Darling, you are my open door, so let's close it indefinitely to all wicked and evil people.

Michelle
March 03, 2015

Where do I start Good God because this world has changed? Man – humans have done all to undo all that you've built.

Many days I want to quit; have told you I am done. I don't want and need you anymore but you stayed. You stayed with me despite me taking out all my anger on you.

Father and God you are the true healer and as March 4th approaches, please tell me what to do.

I've faced hell. Came into this land on this day and death did try to take my life on this day, but I am standing with you. You saved me hence I have to be truly devoted to truth, honesty and cleanliness; You.

Father God stay my death infinitely and indefinitely without end.

I need to be with you not man. Hence let me return to you whole; in the spirit and flesh – human form.

Lovey let evil be over now. Send no one else to rescue humanity after this but truly let it be done so that true peace and happiness can reign on land and in the spiritual realm.

Let the choice of man – humanity be.

Billions did not choose you so you have to let humanity be due to the decisions they've made.

Sin; death is the choice of man – humanity, so let their decision stand because death is truly not you.

You have to give them their forever ever choice hence you cannot stand in the way of death anymore. You cannot continue to feed shelter and clothe wicked and evil people. You have to let them go because they belong to death and I've told you this. You are the one to continue with the pain of self and the ones that have chosen you and this is not right. You are wrong because although you love us so, your loving us so is truly not true. I've told you, true love does not hurt. Love hurts but true love cannot hurt and you know this. True love is not intentional pain, nor does true love do anything intentional to hurt anyone.

Lovey, loneliness is there for me. Pain is there and no one should be lonely. Hence I ask you again to ordain the right someone for me.

How can you say you love us so and let us stay lonely and unfed?

How can you say you are there for us but yet fail to lock away all facet of evil from us?

How can you say you love us so and leave us to live amongst wicked and evil people continuously?

Yes I have many questions and although I am devoted to truth and true love; you, I cannot comprehend you on certain days. Evil should not surround me nor should evil knock at my door.

I should not be hindered but yet I am and this is truly not fair to me. You allow this hindrance and expect me to be happy when I am not. So tell me if you do this to me, how fair and just are you?

Are you not saying you don't want to rescue your children and you could not care less about us?

Look at the true goodness I have for you. So why can't you have this true goodness for me and your children globally?

Take sexual gratification out of all of this. If it happens then so be it, but I need a true friend to do things with. Yes I know you are there and we are limited because you are not human. Sad yes but it's true. Yes I know one day but I hope that day comes soon.

My Darling and True Friend, I need you hence I am asking you to truly open my eyes so that I can see you and be with you.

Stop disappointing me because I truly do not disappoint you.

My good and true choice is you, so why can't it be this way with me and your people continuously?

Yes I know I have to talk to you in this way on the days I feel this way, but it does not help me any.

You should not have to walk away from your people come on now.

You should be there despite our pains and I know you are there but it seems like you're on a vacation since my LA trip and it should not be so. You should be there for me all the time, so truly stop hiding from me because I know when you are there and right now you are truly not there.

Michelle

Yes I know I can't give up. I know I have to continue on my journey but Good God did you have to make it so hard for me?

Did you have to make the road so rough that I want to leave you?

Did you have to make my road and journey so lonely?

Lovey in life we all need encouragement. I need it.

I need to hold on to someone when I am weak. Yes I have you but how many days or how many times have you touched me; hugged me for me to feel you?

Lovey true and good emotion; feel is important to me.

I need to feel you daily but you are not there. Yes there are days that I am encouraged but why can't this be face to face?

Why can't I hug you in my present state face to face?

You're important to me and yes the spirit gets down because I can't touch you; have you my way and I don't think it's fair.

Maybe it's me but I truly do love you.

Yes I am in a world filled with sin; wicked and evil people and I feel helpless when it comes to you.

My emotions are over the place and filled with doubt sometimes and this should truly not be. I cannot take the yoyo emotions anymore. I should not feel this way but yet I do and it's weird. No one should feel like a yoyo emotionally with you.

If you are there for me and your people, truly be there for us. My intentions are truly good for you when it comes to you and our people come on now.

Save us and stop it with the yoyo emotions. I have to stop also hence we must take doubt permanently out of our way more than infinitely and indefinitely.

I truly don't want to lose you so why are you allowing evil to take you from me and your people? And you cannot say this isn't so because all I have to do is point at the sins of man – humanity. Our sins hinder you so yes in many ways we hinder you too. The blame is squarely not on you but on us also. I know you cannot come into a dirty planet or home but Good God, why can't you make it easy for us to clean up self and planet and truly walk with you?

We need you but how can we have you when sin surrounds us and you have not told me how to clean spirit and self; body?

Lovey I know you can connect to me and with me so why do you not do this each and every day?

We all need wisdom and overstanding; You but yet we truly do not have you. At least I don't have you the way I want and need to have you.

So truly tell me now. Why should you be taken from me?

Why can't I enjoy you?
Why do I have to share you?

Yes I know I have to but on this day I don't want to. I want and need you for myself.

Yes this is me sometimes and I am so not going to change. So from time to time Lovey, encourage me like I encourage you.

Keep strong and safe because I know I will be home soon.

Michelle

Ah Good God can someone dedicate I CAN SEE by Christopher Martin to me?

Can they serenade me in true love with this song?

Oh Lovey if only this can be for me and you too?

Wow.

Could we not be meant to be like this?

Ah Darling, this is you and me, so I dedicate this song to you endlessly.

Michelle

Oh Lord have mercy because I have to interrupt this book and dedicate GIVE IT ALL YOU GOT by Beres Hammond to you.

Truly accept this from me to you and give it all you got today before it's too late.

My Darling our hearts are pure and as I seek you let me truly find you.

Let me truly have you before I get too old and grey.

Darling, you are my sun that is shining for you.

So baby give it all you got today because my true and good will is for you.

And because I more than unconditionally truly love you more than infinitely and indefinitely, I am going to give you all that I got. I need to follow my mind and truly find you on this day.

True love always My Darling.

Michelle and Michelle Jean

The good part of like is knowing that you are truly loved; cared for.

The sad part is knowing that negative energy surrounds us.

For some we are hindered from doing all that is good and true and this is sad. Sad to know that wicked and evil spirit and people dominate and control this earth.

Sad to know that evil refuses to relinquish its hold on humanity – society.

Sad to know that all that evils said he would do to humanity evil did. And now for billions it's truly too late.

The ways of the wicked control and dominate; dictate and it's sad but this is man's reality. We give up life for death and surely including shortly humanity will pay the price for their disobedience; sins.

Michelle

Dear God – Good God it's March 04, 2015 and the power is out.

God where have you been?
I mean what is the purpose of life when life can be taken away at will?

What is the purpose of you saying you love us so when life isn't valued by humans?

Today I have many questions because life has failed me. Meaning you've abandoned us in so many ways.

Were you just in doing this?

I say yes because of our sins. But as some of us move towards cleanliness you, you need to encourage; change.

You need to let your people know that you are there for them.

How can we come home when we have no direction?

How can we come home when there's no happiness; true love with us and amongst us?

Can a father or mother say they care and let their children run free?

Yes I know death's children run free and you do not do this, but where is your care for the few that look to you?

Where is your care for the few that you truly call your own and want to come home to you?

Should you not be preparing a place for them?

Why should they live amongst wicked and evil people?

Lovey, "the wages of sin is death," but where is the truth in you for your people?

Should you not be securing them now?

Yes we are devoted but if you don't clean the mess out of your house and or home, how is your home going to become clean?

I need a clean home hence I have to clean house. I have to ensure that my life is okay in all that I do.

I cannot worry about wicked and evil people including children anymore.

Yes I know the reason why you left us to fend for ourselves. I see the disobedience and I too want to move on from my children. A parent can only talk so much before they say fuck it and leave. I am at that stage with mine. I have too much financial hardships; burdens and they don't seem to care.

Schooling is an issue for them because they don't care about their future. They don't wake up in time to go to school and I am tired of waking them up.

No matter how hard you push, if a child or anyone set them self up for failure they will fail.

Grant you many are not like this, many try and fail. But this is not failure to me; the right door has not opened for you yet. Many take years to get a break and yes many give up like me at times. But I still keep going no matter the odds against me.

I know I was set to fail hence family is a bitch sometimes. Thus good and true, honest and clean people are truly hard to find. Yes I get down on you a lot Good God because true friends I truly don't have a part from you but that's okay. I stay to myself and truly bug you. You are my true friend hence I worry not about man – humanity and the crap that they do.

All I ask is for you to make this the final call for man – humanity because the pain has gone on for far too long. Nor does humanity respect you.

They trust lies over you and this is so not fair nor is it right when it comes to you.

You give us all but yet we are so ungrateful and wicked to you. After all you've given us we turn from you and praise someone else over you.

You gave us so much in abundance but yet we pollute the abundance you've given us. Changed the abundance you've given us. Now look at the diseases that plague man due to the polluted foods we eat and the polluted water we drink.

My Darling, I need to rest and I am resting now because I am not seeing as much disaster. But you have to truly do better for my sake and your good and true people's sake.

As humans we cannot continue to hate because in many ways we are truly not all the same.

Yes there is sexual perversion out there but Good God, what is true love to you?

Michelle

Good God the way I truly love is that okay with you?

The way I talk to you and hold you dear to me, is that okay?

Tell me something Good God, if the wages of sin is death, why is sin in our genes?

If the world was to end tomorrow or today, would you still choose me?

Would you spend my last hours, minutes and seconds with me?

Would you hold me and truly shield me from the storm and storms that come my way; death?

Tell me Good God, why do we have will?

Should you not take all sin from us if we request it?

Remember the spirit is total energy and water can clean the spirit thoroughly. So why isn't the waters of earth washing our spirit clean?

And please don't tell me it's because as humans we pollute everything including the waterways.

I truly don't need excuses Good God. I need truth, your true all all the way.

MY MANY QUESTIONS TO GOD

We know that evil kill and destroy, so why is evil here on earth?

Do you not know about care and the way I care about you?

Lovey let wicked and evil people go and secure the future of those who care about you and truly love you. The end is near yes and I feel as if you've abandoned me.

Safety is not the issue. It's like you've become silent. You've left me in the dark and although I can see I feel as if there is something truly missing between us.

Tell me something Lovey, when does true goodness come to me?

When does truth truly reign down to earth?

Yes we have our security measures but what good are they if nations know not them; you?

Lovey I truly don't know because none of this makes any sense to me. You are my flag of life but yet, why isn't my flag truly with me?

Michelle

How do I describe this feel Good God?

I yearn to go away again.
Yearn to go to Cayman or Russia.

Yes I need to take the train from Russia to China and back or vise versa.

My Darling I need you.
Need the scenery of life.

My Darling you are my hope and I need to enjoy you.

Ah Lovey truly forgive me of all my sins everywhere.

Forgive me if I've failed you but in all I do, I have to stand up for truth and justice.

I have to think of you and others – your good and true people.

Ah Lovey where's our true peace?

Where's our hope for a better future; tomorrow?

Yes we love each other true, but why can't our true love heal and fix all that is broken with man, the earth, environment and universe?

My Darling why do we continue to be broken?

Why can't we fix all that is broken between us?

Why do we continue to stay apart?

Should we not be joined in goodness and in truth?

Should we not rise and heal all who needs healing globally? Meaning heal all the good people globally who needs healing. They need healing too Good God so why can't we do all that is good and true for them?

Should we not rise and provide a good and true home globally?

Should we not squash all sin and sins and make the environment we live in truly whole and clean?

Michelle and Michelle Jean

Good God why is the hearts of men so corrupt?

Why do we live for corruption and sin?

Lovey, let me take council with you because something is truly not right between me and you.

Yes you are the light and way but why darkness? Yes I know the light in the darkness but there has to be more.

I know about death.
I know about life; you but in all I do, I truly do not know you it seems. Look at it, the devil give his and her people all they want to keep them with him and her but what do you do?

You give but we truly can't receive because your giving is spiritual and not physical on some levels and this is truly sad. Yes the spiritual life is it, but what about the physical life?

Do we not need reassurance here too?

Do we not need you on the physical level as well?

How can you be our morning dew when our blessings; morning dew is being taken away?

MY MANY QUESTIONS TO GOD

Why should your true people be constantly bank rolled and blacklisted by death and their children and people? Come on now.

Why do we not matter to you?

Why should we be alone all the time?

Yes I have many questions. Many yearnings but yet with all this said, things go unanswered with you. So if this is the case, how are we going to learn and know the truth of you?

Why are you hiding you?

Why are you being like a deadbeat dad; father?

With all this said, you have failed to show me your true world.

I need a new beginning with you but what good is life if I truly cannot see you and your world. I know the world of death; seen it too but you; with you things are different. I cannot see you or see into your world. Hence you cannot be one way and or one sided Good God come on now.

Death shows me him and her but yet you hide from me. Now I have to ask you, what is the purpose of you hiding from me? No, I should stop this because it seems I've forgotten you've shown me you as female in the physical realm. You've shown me you are inside of me.

You've shown me you as an open door. So please forgive me because you did show me you. I am the one to have forgotten. So let me stop this line of questioning because I've become a little forgetful and this is truly wrong. So let me get back on track by saying My Darling it's March 04, 2015 and this date is significant to me and you, but yet it feels like you are gone from me.

Lovey what's truly wrong? Death should no longer have a hold on me. I need involvement in a good and true way. So truly come back to me and truly stop being one sided. You cannot show all about death and show nothing about you. We need to know about you and your world.

Michelle

MY MANY QUESTIONS TO GOD

Dear God what are the people of this world coming to?

No one is safe.
Too much happening hence the lies many tell.

Michelle
March 04, 2015

Many questions are there to be asked Good God but on this day I don't want to leave things alone.

I need answers and I need you to give them to me.

Good God you cannot leave us hanging nor can you leave us standing alone holding any empty bag.

Everyone has made promises when it comes to you and cannot deliver and this has to stop.

You cannot give us empty promises to live on. These empty promises are like shattered glass. They are broken and they do cut and cause us to bleed if we step on them. You are not this way I know but it feels as if you are.

There's so many things I want and need to do with you but yet I cannot do and this is wrong.

Yes we need to know you on all levels but we can't. All we see and know is evil and I will not settle for this.

If this is a test then you are infinitely wrong because no one should have to feel pain to be with the one they truly love.

True love is not about pain nor does it cause pain intentionally.

My way with you is my choice. I have no true and devoted friend but you and I need it to stay this way indefinitely. The loneliness here on earth for me and with me is brutal and this is why I bug you for a good and true mate. I hide nothing from you and you shouldn't either.

Michelle

Good God how can you say you love us so and watch us die like this?

Does that make any sense?

You love us so but yet you continue to let us live in sin and amongst sinful and wicked people.

You say you love us so but yet have done nothing positive or constructive to rid the earth and or world of all that is wicked and evil.

You say you love us so but yet leave us to die amongst the wicked and evil.

You continue to let us bury our good dead in the cemeteries of the wicked; dead.

Darling, My Darling as physical good must be separated from the physical wicked and evil you must separate spiritual good from the spiritual and evil also. No don't smile because you know I would want and need this also.

I cannot be your child, devoted and true love if I did not think of the spiritual good also.

Oh Dear God I have to interrupt my writing for this book. It's March 08, 2015 and as I write this book my spirit and or energy feels drained; as if my energy is draining from me. This book isn't difficult to write but something is being taken from me while I write this book.

It's as if the spirit is weakened; dying.

Lovey why?

I am not lost but the spirit is truly weak right now. Hence I truly don't know who is going to die in my family but I am feeling the pangs of death. I know when a person's leaf fall off the tree of life death does not come right away. And yes I know it doesn't have to be someone in my family that is going to die but my energy is being drained and it feels horrible in a way. Hence I tell people the closest they will get to death in the living is sickness. Yes I have to continue on with this book. When I finish is another story and chapter.

Oh God I feel so drained. On times like these I wish I had true people around me that could give me strength to go on. True people that can comprehend what I am going through and encircle me with good true and clean prayer. Man I thought death was done with me but I guess not. Somehow I feel like a conduit of some kind for death and the world of death. Oh well I guess I have to go through it.

Onwards I go.

Lovey come on now. You know me and my desire for justice all around. I truly need you so why would I not do good unto you? Yes NO WEAPONS FORMED AGAINST ME SHALL PROSPER. Thank you Mr. Fred Hammond on this day because I need TOTAL PRAISE AND STRENGTH.

Yes Good God I am your good and true defender, but truly loving you is not all. Well yes it is but there is more to me and you truly know this.

So in all that we do, we must fight for justice. Meaning we must be victorious at all time (s) when it comes to injustice.

Wicked can no longer roam and take at will because evil did lose in 2013 and I will forever remind you of this.

Michelle and Michelle Jean

Okay Good God it's March 05, 2015 and I have to ask you what did I miss?

What fault did you find in my devotion and praise to you?

What hate am I spreading?

Lovey according to my dream this morning my biological father dropped me off at the airport. He dropped me off at gate 8 (eight) and I spent 2 – 3 hours at gate 8 (eight) and when I got inside to check in, I realized I was at the wrong gate. I should have been at gate 5 (five). Yes I had many things with me and it was impossible for me to carry them alone. So this white lady helped me with my belongings to get them checked. Upon realizing I was at the wrong gate, I left gate eight and went to gate five but I missed the flight so it seems. Yes there is more to the dream like this white man that I seem to know and the lack of help by my own black people.

Alright Lovey because I truly don't want to go ballistic on you because it seems you want to anger me and you know for a fact that you do not have my temper. Mine is worse than yours because not even hell can contain me when I get angry at you. You of yourself can't calm me down and contain me.

I truly love you but if you drop me off at the wrong gate will I not be lost; be late for my true destination?

Now tell me, will I not miss our flight like in the dream? So why the hell are you dropping me off at the wrong gate; gate number eight?

Listen My Darling; I refuse to hate any Babylonian. I refuse to spread hate, so truly hear me and never ever drop me off at gate eight (8) again. This is not my gate nor is it my number. I am not Babylonian. They spread hate because they are lodged at gate 8 (eight) and I refuse more than wholeheartedly to hate (8) anyone. I need not have to remind you of this gate and my dream of the Babylonian woman and the number 8 (eight).

I refuse to hate and I refuse to hate them. I did not make any provision for them and it's going to stay this way indefinitely because the lie caused Eve (Evening) her life and place with you. The lie also caused some of our ancestors their life in the wilderness with Mother Moses. Duly remember the golden calf that our ancestors accepted and danced around according to the Illuminati Book of Death – man's so called holy bible.

<u>The cow is Death. It is fire and every Judahite that is of you and true to you know this.</u>

Jamaicans know this hence we were forbidden to marry them. (The Babylonians)

You know this hence I refuse to spread hate. I have to tell the truth; total truth and this is why I tell you to never ever let any of the words in these books spread hate. I refuse to hate them. Negative energy is them not me.

They lie and steal.

They cheat and steal your identity and I refuse to lie and steal anyone's identity.

<u>I do not need their culture nor do I need their nasty hair. Other nasty black people can put dem what lef inna fi dem head but not me. There is absolutely nothing beautiful about them, so why the bleep would I want to be like them. I am blessed and highly favoured, so why would I give up my blessings for a culture and or cultures of death? Come on now.</u>

I also told you no one should use any of the words in this book to spread hate. If they do, take from them their portion in your good and true world. Yes take your Breath of Life from them. <u>I refuse hate because I know the hurt and pain hate cause.</u> Humanity has the truth and they must now live by the truth. So if I am missing your mark and flight then whose fault is that?

MY MANY QUESTIONS TO GOD

Are you not teaching wrong and delivering wrong?

Yes I am putting you in the mix because I've told you of my good and true intentions and will and you are not listening to me. So truly stop because you are pissing me off.

Why the hell would I want to lose my place with you?

Have I not devoted myself to Goodness and Truth; You?

Have I not devoted myself to good and clean life?

Do I not truly love you more than infinitely and indefinitely forever ever more than unconditionally, so where does the problem lie?

You need full truth; total truth and I've given that to you unconditionally.

I've told you my greatest fear is losing you hence I ask you for impenetrable frameworks and foundations when it comes to us and all that we do that is good and true.

Lovey, what more can I offer you of me? Come on now. You are my truth, so why would I spread hate?

When I do this, I would not be true to you and I refuse to let you take my truth and integrity from me. If you see someone else then go in truth to them but do not insult me like this.

You want to hate by all means go ahead, but truly do not bring me in your hate bullshit.

I've told you the total truth must be told and I refuse to spread hate doing it. I refuse and you cannot make me go against my good and true will.

My truth and true love of you is more than valued. It is priceless, so truly let go of your hate bullshit because I will level you with my anger and you know this. You are important to me and you complete me but I will not stand you doubting me when it comes to hate.

Truly look at the earth globally and the hate that is amongst man and in man and I'm to continue with this bullshit?

No, I refuse to.

If you want to walk away from me because I do not spread hate go; go in peace not pieces because I will truly devour you.

MY MANY QUESTIONS TO GOD

Many people have and has lost their lives due to lies and hate and I refuse to prolong and or carry on the hate trend. I refuse to. We all belong you know this. It's our sins that take us from you and I refuse to take myself from goodness and truth; You. So truly stop dropping me off at the wrong gate.

Yes I know you had to do this. Show me gate 8 but I refuse GATE 8 (HATE). There is absolutely no place in our world for this gate. So tell Babylon to kiss my natural brown ass and their hate (8) bullshit. They are bleeping haters because I refuse to come their way.

Lovey, mi fi gi yu up?

Listen do not fuel my anger because giving you up is not an option. As for him close that gate if that is not the right gate for me to go. I refuse to lose you because of a male and or shirt.

I've told you, you are important to me and I will not intentionally hurt you. Yes I will say things to piss you off for you to listen and hear me. Hence I rely on you for true sight; my sight. Yes at times I decipher wrong and I am sorry for this hence we have to be more solid and true in the sight department.

I refuse to lose my sight because I value this gift from you. So truly know me and trust me; yes cherish me.

Tell me something, why give me your last name and receive me under your order if you cannot trust and cherish me?

Yes I know you trust me and this is your way of pissing me off and showing these evil Babylonians; Death that I am true to you and that I come to you with all – everything.

Yes I know evil gets to you too but I am there for you. You know who and what I truly love; I cherish and I do cherish you and all that you do for me.

<u>Listen Lovey, I cannot go on the hate train nor WILL I PUT ENMITY BETWEEN THEM AND US; SATAN'S SEED AND OUR SEED. I refuse to do this because no form of hate is worth it. Hate destroys; kill and I refuse to destroy and kill anyone. Like I've told you what belong to Death let them take it and go in true peace. They cannot disturb our true peace and tranquility anymore.</u> Evil's children have and has been telling you for more than years, decades and centuries that they do not want you. So truly listen and let death's children dem guh. You are not their choice and you have to live with their decision. You have the true loves of your life already so truly save your people. And yes I am interrupting the flow of what I've written.

MY MANY QUESTIONS TO GOD

Lovey, you have more than true love in me and with me so truly enjoy it and me. Yes I know you want to save the Black Race but the Black Race based on hue have told you time and time again that they don't want you so leave dem. Mek dem continue to suffa. Look pan mi an mi pickney dem. Mi want what's best for them but some refuse to listen, suh mi a guh walk and lef dem to the choice and choices they've made. <u>**I WILL NOT GO TO THE SLAUGHTER HOUSE OF DEATH WITH THEM. NOR WILL I GO TO THE SLAUGHTER HOUSE OF DEATH FOR THE BLACK RACE COME ON NOW.**</u> Baby I have you, so why should I disrespect you and abandon you.

Look at this way. I am on Twitter and many people pay a fee for people to follow them. Why the hell should I do this?

I should not have to pay people to follow me come on now. You are not death nor do you say follow me. Those you choose to deliver your message you stay with them forever ever. When you leave us we are the ones to do something wrong. <u>**You gave us all that is good and true so why should you have to pay the price to maintain and sustain DUTTY PEOPLE, come on now.**</u>

You are Good God so why should you have to put up with dirty and unclean people?

DEATH PAY TO KEEP PEOPLE COMING TO HIM HENCE THE TIDES AND OFFERINGS PEOPLE PAY DEATH TO KILL THEM. (RELIGION AND THE CHURCHES OF ALL FACET OF DEATH).

YOU ARE NOT DEATH HENCE YOU REQUIRE NO PAYMENT FROM ANYONE. COME ON NOW

You are the truth hence you are everlasting life. I know this but the rest of humanity does not.

Am I laughing all the way to the bank?

Yes because I have you. You are my bank roll and payroll. Yes Human Resources Manager.

Onwards I go because you are my black card and more than infinite good and true bank accounts. Hence I have to bank my all (goodness and truth, cleanliness and honesty plus) in you.

Listen Lovey, I cannot go on the hate train hence I tell you separate Good from All that is Wicked and Evil. Trust me I truly do not need to be around hateful people. I will not and cannot prosper with them.

Listen. No remember what my son said to me March 04, 2015. He said he would never listen to me because he has

his life mapped out already and I cannot tell him anything. He won't listen.

This is fine. He's made his decision in life. I cannot hate him for this because it's his life. I have to move on now because I will never prosper with this child. The spirit clashes and my spirit want to run from him.

He's the prodigal son but trust me I have no interest in prodigal sons or daughters. I have to do what is right for me and you and the good and true seeds you've given me. If a child don't want good council you leave them like you did Eve (Evening), let them fend for themselves on their own. Yes I would provide for them like you did Eve (Evening) but true help she no longer have because she died. She did not listen to you nor did she heed your good council. She chose death over you hence she lived with death and in death. This had nothing to do with colour of skin. Death is death not clean. She did not want clean life and she got what she wanted because she did choose death over you and I refuse to do this again. I have a second chance with you and despite my nagging and negative ways, I am trusting you to keep me glued to you all when mi sey mi nuh want yu and yu fi let mi goh.

I truly don't want to leave you hence I truly have to do for you. You know my yoyo emotions.

Hence I need my emotions to be more than solid in you. I don't need the bipolar effect anymore.

Too stressful and annoying. And don't you dare say I'm annoying whilst smiling down at me.

Remember you are my yesterday, today and tomorrow and I truly don't want or need to lose you.

So in all you do, take hate from my DNA – Genes.

Listen we all have a choice and humanity has and have made their choice. My choice is the good and true you; truth, goodness and honesty; cleanliness and it's going to stay this way.

Michelle and Michelle Jean

Ah Lovey I'm a big deal when it comes to you because I am truly proud of you. As I think of you I cannot lose sight of your values and truth.

As humans we have choices hence I must live by your guidelines and law.

I have to live by the laws of you as seen on the mountain because I know who your true race and people are.

I cannot buy into the diversity bullshit because hell is real and it's not everyone on the face of the planet that belong (s) to you. Some races are not included on your mountain hence I've made no provision for them more than infinitely and indefinitely forever ever.

Is this wrong?

No because truth is everlasting life and many are truly not truthful.

I know Islam and the lies and hate they spread.
I know the True Jews.
I know the Babylonians Jews (Israelites) and the lies they tell on you. **HENCE THE UPRIGHT AND DOWNWARD TRIANGLE MUST NEVER EVER BE INTERLOCKED – UNITED.**

Yes this goes for Males and Females. Meaning as your children we're not to procreate and or interlock and or unite with wicked and evil; unclean men and women. We were to keep within our realm of cleanliness and this is why it is permissible for women to lay with women and men to lay with men. But the way society is they've forgotten the truth and cleanliness of you. We bash each other and put enmity; strife between this person and the next person.

Likes are to stay true to likes and unlike are to stay true to unlike. Hence evil cannot change. Evil must seek and destroy; kill everything in its path. Thus evil is pure and negative energy.

Evil cannot be clean it will always be dirty.

Life hath nothing to do with death so truly woe be unto those Jews that marry death and call spiritual death (Islam) their friend.

That way of life (Islam) was and still is condemned and I will not make any way for any Babylonian. The accepting death trend must stop and it stops with me. I refuse all Babylonian (s) hence Islam (spiritual death) and all facets of Religion (Death) is rejected and condemned by me more than infinitely and indefinitely forever ever without end.

And for those who truly don't know. Christianity is also death. (Physical Death)

I give them (no Babylonian; death) no way in to you and our kingdom Good God because I know your pain and hurt. The lies that was told to (Eve) Evening for her to give up her life and place with you. Good God she toiled in pain and hurt and still she could not come back to you. She died and I truly don't want or need this for me and you. Nor do I want and need this for our good and true people.

Lovey finding you was not easy and I truly don't want to lose you. Like I've told you, all when mi sey goh, nuh goh du. Truly nuh goh.

<u>WITHOUT YOU LIFE IS DEATH; OUR LIFE IS DEAD. WE VOID OUR CHANCE AND LIFE WITH YOU ONCE WE GIVE YOU UP AND I TRULY CANNOT AFFORD THIS. I CANNOT GIVE MY LIFE UP TO GO LIVE A WUSSERRA LIFE IN HELL. NO COME ON NOW.</u>

The Ethiopians did this bullshit long before Eve (Evening) hence there is a hatred there for them by you. And yes I've said you do not hate but I asked the question using the word hate and he showed me why.

He did not tell me, he showed me. He showed me his shoes. Meaning Ethiopia was a holy place and they were not to walk on your land with their shoes and they did. They walked in your holy place with their dirty shoes and for this you have a more than a bone to pick with them because good and true; clean life began in this land and they did the unthinkable by trampling you down with their dirty shoes. So yes, that's one BLACK NATION THAT GAVE YOU UP FOR THE BABYLONIAN EMPIRE AND THIS IS WHY YOU CAN FIND BLACKS IN BABYLON (INDIA) UNTIL THIS DAY.

Another Black land sold you out as well. America, the United States of America also rejected you because Life came to Life (Marcus Garvey) and they rejected him. My homeland (Jamaica) did the same thing. JUDAH WHORED JUST LIKE THEIR SISTER ISRAEL. Instead of walking away from the original turncoats and sellouts, Judah readily accepted them and say that FRAUD SELASSIE IS THEIR GOD.

ISRAEL'S GOD CAN NEVER BE JUDAH'S GOD BECAUSE YOU GOOD GOD AND ALLELUJAH KNOW NOT ISRAEL. They sold you out originally

hence you left them alone. Israel represent death hence the interlocking flag of death. They show you that they are death, have accepted death because this star is the star of death. This star is in the church and churches of death. Hence the death star that humanity has and have forgotten about. And yes this is why the churches do not speak of the planet (s) of death because they know not about them.

Like I said, we all have choice (s) and the black race based on hue have been accepting death for far too long while selling you out in the process. Each time you send your true messenger to save them, they reject you. So truly leave them alone because you did show me the headstones and grave sight of them. Hence "hell is full of black people and recruiting more." ***Islam***

The hurtful part of all of this is, knowing how lowly we've become; fallen to the point where every race globally hates us and want to destroy us. But in truth Good God can you blame them?

Good God we sell you out and expect you to just get up and let us in just like that. Our forefathers and mothers disgraced you; turned from you and accepted death. Now look at how many have and has accepted spiritual death Islam in the living.

LOOK HOW MANY HAVE CHANGED THEIR BIOLOGICAL NAMES TO ACCEPT THE LAST AND FIRST NAME OF DEATH?

Look how many have and has accepted the languages of Babylon (death).

Babylon fell yes but in truth Babylon did not fall under Nimrod – the Black Devil. He commissioned his demonic people to spread the language of hate (the devil) globally and this is why they were scattered. Now look at the world and some black nations loving the languages of the devil and his people. (Sanscript, Farsi, Urdu, Arabic Phoenician). Please these languages are not of you and I know this.

Death's people did their jobs hence the religions and languages of the world. Every nation have and has been influenced by Death and no one can say otherwise because all I have to do is point to our sins, the wars of men throughout the ages, the blood that is being shed on land. More recently in Russia, Nemstov. So no one can tell me shit. Bleep diversity because death is not diverse. Death kills hence death's children murder and capture some of your lands. Yes it's not always the case because they have your personal information and every cent they take from your bank account that you don't notice adds up. Does fuel and fund their war and hate games.

Keep your bleeping immigration, immigration reforms and policies because in my world and kingdom that is good and true, every child of Satan and his cohorts (agents), demons of hell and earth; the physical and spiritual realm including the universe and places I have not mentioned is more than infinitely and indefinitely locked out more than forever ever without end indefinitely.

Keep your bullshit of lies and deceit; hate and death. I have self worth for myself, my people and the god that I more than unconditionally truly love.

Keep your hell because life; true life is more important than death. Keep your fires and keep dancing and walking around it too. (fire). I have the waters of goodness and cleanliness of Good God and Allelujah already. So why the hell would I want you and your decaying and broken world?

Michelle

So Good God if anyone say I am racist so be it because I am in good company. I will not sell you out for death.

Like I've told you, my fear is losing you and I refuse to lose you.

Death is not my choice. My good and true desire is life – good and true life and it's going to stay this way. Hence I do my best to stay away from wicked and evil people.

<u>Goodness is my choice. Life – Good and True Life hath no end but Death hath an end.</u>

I do not want us to end so why would I choose to die; go to hell and die?

Lovey, my life is important so would I give it away falsely to death?

Sweetie big up yuself. Laugh

Bleep the devil and death, his children too. You're good to go so truly love you.

Michelle

Lovey I am not going to let my dream get to me because I am saying my peace to you.

No matter the frozen red or pink fish (salmon), no matter me being dropped off at gate number 8 at the airport; despite me dreaming about LA, despite me having leaves (flowers and some with thorns (sharp points)), despite me dreaming about my sister and her daughter it matters not to me.

And yes despite me seeing him and him in some way reminding me of the demon that was in my life. Trust me I was reminded of him in the living but he failed to kill me. I am still standing because I was saved. Hence I look to thee Good God for all.

Death targeted me in the living and spiritual and I'm still standing giving you praise and doubt Lovey. I am still a torn in your side. Well beside you. You My Darling and True Love is my BIG DEAL AND YOU ARE VERY IMPORTANT TO ME.

Michelle

Lovey and Good God truly protect me. Encourage me because I need your encouragement today.

As I seek please be there for me in a good and true way.

Please do not be disappointed in me but accept me for who I am.

Accept me with all my faults; well flaws.

Lovey today I need you and others hence I am coming to you also for strength, good and true encouragement. And as I hold on to you see me and put your arms around me.

Sweetheart my body is being drained right now. I feel as if I am going in circles with our books and it should not be this way.

Why can't we be stable and true to each other?

Why can't things be easy for me and you for a change? I am doing all to listen and move on but I can't seem to find the right road with you why?

I feel confused and all alone.
Cannot comprehend why this is still happening to me.

I do not want to continue to be on the wrong road if I am on the wrong road Good God.

Oh God this book is draining me spiritually and physically and I cannot comprehend this. Is this supposed to happen to me?

As I look to you for guidance truly guide me and protect me because I truly need you in my life and in all that I do.

Lovey, please hear me and truly help me because I feel as if I am failing you and me. No, I do not feel this way on this day but there are days when I feel this way.

I feel all the forces of negativity – Death is hindering me from getting the truth out there.

Lovey, help me to truly stop this. Help me to stop the forces of death and their people from hindering me.

Michelle

I've made it over the hurdle Good God so why is evil hindering me and the truth of you and me?

Lovey maybe it's me.

Maybe I need to stop writing and find another avenue.

Maybe, maybe, maybe.
I need to stop this because when you are walking on the pathway of truth nothing comes easy when it comes to wicked and evil people including spirits.

Ah Lovey on this day I am down because I feel as if I have chosen the wrong road to represent me.

She did say to go to NYC and I am doing so but why does it have to be so hard?

Lovey, truly deliver me because it's not an easy road for me.

My road is hard and filled with many pitfalls but somehow I am encouraged no matter how I feel unencouraged.

I have to continue to let you be my good choice and all. I just hope you now keep me from falling.

I need you Lovey so please let me find the right road to you and with you.

Lovey I so want to cry on this day but I have to hold back the tears.

Yes it's getting harder for me financially but it's okay. I am prepared to fall and lose it all. I will not fight any more financially because I truly have no more fight left in me financially.

I have to face reality and if this is to be let it be so because it was truly ordained by you.

Yes I refuse to accept defeat but you have to when you are defeated, and I am financially and emotionally defeated.

Ah My Darling stay cool because one day I will build you our 25 million dollar mega mansion if not purchase it for you.

Michelle and Michelle Jean

Ah God, Good God I am on the verge of tears. My life has become boring and I so want to get out of the house.

My nature is creeping up on me and it's pretty bad but I have to try to contain myself.

Why Good God?
Why is my nature so painful?
Hard on my body?

I don't want to lay with just anyone and have sex. Yes I am being picky because I truly don't want to disappoint you. Eight years and counting Lovey and I truly can't go anymore. I have to stop and think about my celibacy issues. I have to do what's right for me right now.

Yes I think of you and disappointing you but my body is in pain. I can't hold out any longer and you know this.

Good God why does anyone have to live this way?

Why do I live in fear of disappointing you sexually?

Lovey can you please do something about this? I truly don't want to make the wrong decision but yet in a way I want to be defiant.

I am tired of being disappointed by people and to some degree you.

I keep asking and you keep failing me in the loneliness department. So what do you leave us to do?

Do you not leave us to fail you; make the wrong choice and decision?

Yes opportunity is there, but is this what you want for me? Lovey I truly don't know.

Yes I am bored of staying at home and you are so not opening any doors for me, so what do I truly do?

Doors are closed to me and right now I am down in the dumps.

Maybe tomorrow will be a better day where my nature isn't riding me so much.

Michelle

Ah Good God what's going on?

If the Jews – true Jews have the word to make Islam – evil flee, why are we not using this word Good God?

Why are we not causing all facets of evil to flee?

Why is evil still here on the face of this planet – earth?

Why is death still around?

Lovey and Good God, why do I not have this word?

No I do. Truth and good will towards you and our people hence I plea with you to separate good – all good from all facets of evil infinitely and indefinitely forever ever without end where ever evil reside (s).

My true more than true love of you is more than my stay hence I come to you with everything. But still Good God, why isn't the true Jews doing what they are supposed to do? The earth needs to be cleansed of all evil and we have to use your word to get rid of it.

<u>Lovey everyone has learnt lies but how many have and has learnt the truth?</u>

<u>How many of us can tell the truth?</u>

Some say they want the truth and when they get it they can't handle it. They shy away from it.

So what's the point of asking for the truth if you can't handle it? You are self centered and one way; linear.

Life does not revolve around one person, it revolves around us all.

Lovey, I have the truth of you hence truth is everlasting life. So yes I will use the truth which is the word to shatter and scatter all evil from around us and our people. I have to know the full truth so when the devil come to eat up my flesh and spirit they more than stumble in their own pits of hell and deceit.

Those who do not want to know the truth of you which is true love can go. I refuse to hate anyone nor will I put enmity between anyone. The South is your land and it is going to stay this way because positive energy and life cannot hurt anyone. I will not concern myself about them (wicked and evil people including wicked and evil spirits). I truly have you Good God and it's going to stay this way infinitely and indefinitely forever ever without end.

Michelle and Michelle Jean

My Darling and King rise with me in truth and harmony; goodness and cleanliness.

Help me to build you as well as build you your 25 million dollar mega mansion right away.

Dear Lord, Lovey and King – True King, give me your word of truth now so that I can cause all facet of Islam and Religion to flee from man – your true people infinitely and indefinitely more than forever ever without end.

The devil and his children, people must flee all our domains and kingdoms of truth and true life more than forever ever without end infinitely and indefinitely.

Dear Lord, Good God and True Friend, I make no provision or provisions for any evil hence no evil regardless of colour, race, creed, religion, ethnicity with the exception of Germans and Babylonians, these two races and or ethnic group I will never ever ever without a shadow of a doubt save. I will save no evil because they are not, truly not our people. I refuse them as I've refused death.

Sorry death but you are not a part of my true world even though I know you. Good God, I know you and if you want to send someone to save these people this is your choice but I will not save them if I am the saving grace for humanity. ***The decision to let people in your kingdom is not mine but yours but truly keep them the hell away from me.*** Hence if you have to, we will design a kingdom for just me and you. You can visit me from time to time but not them.

My good and true choice will always be good and true life for me and you Good God and Allelujah, my good and true family and the good and true seeds you have given me.

I also extend good wishes and good prosperity to China, Kenya, Russia and I truly don't know why Russia but someday I will and the Southern lands of Africa except for South Africa. Yes I remember Nelson Mandela but South Africa has never truly been on my good radar. So whatever you do Good God, truly save Nelson Mandela for me because he did try to help his people truthfully. 27 years he was imprisoned hence truly vindicate him by truly saving him from the pangs of hell. Put him in our Valley of the Kings and let him rest and live in peace forevermore. He truly deserves it Good God. Remember Marcus Mosiah Garvey also and truly save him. Yes I know he's saved but truly remember him and Robert Nesta Marley (Bob Marley).

Michelle

My Darling I have to ask for salvation for these men because they did try to save their people. Their people just did not want saving and this is truly a pity; sad.

Yes I truly love Jamaica but the wickedness of the people I truly do not like or love.

You gave us your name Good God hence we are Judahites; the true Jews. You did separate us but not all Jews – Judahites come from Jamaica. Some reside in Russia hence I will plea the case of all Russian Jews globally.

I know this is strange Lovey because there is so much about the land and people I truly do not know.

Lovey and King, do I have ancestors in that land from the days of old that I truly do not know and or know about?

I know Mongolia – Asia but my full and true history I truly do not know.

I know I am drawn to Russia but why? I know some of their history but the full truth of their past I truly do not know.

Michelle

MY MANY QUESTIONS TO GOD

<u>Good God hear me now and answer my question, but is there an Islamic agenda?</u>

<u>Is all this war that the different nations are involved in a ploy for a hidden Islamic agenda?</u>

Remember my dream and or vision years ago of the Islamic men wanting to marry the Jews.

Lovey, truly answer me because no true Jew can marry a Muslim. It is forbidden by law and by you. Cleanliness Good God cleanliness and truth. I know this, you know this but yet we do it anyway.

Lovey you know if Babylon rise again hell will be unleashed upon earth in a more than brutal way because this time around Babylon will not give up their seat.

If white people based on hum think that Babylon will be loyal to them they had truly better think again because Babylon is only faithful to Babylon; death. So truly good luck to them because the hell they will face here

on earth will be worse than the slavery of the Blacks and Jews combined.

So truly good luck to America and all the lands that give Babylonians a home because I will not save them. "The wages of sin is death," hence the devil's children (Babylonians) are going to let them pay and pay dearly.

Hell is real and many has and have sealed their faith; name in the book of death already. Many don't think that the sacrifice they make unto death, death can take their family members and or a family member if they cannot pay off their loan to death. They fail to realize that the children they have and or adopt belong (s) to death if they have kids. There is absolutely nothing they can do about this because it is in the contract of death.

<u>So for all you black mothers that allow the demon seeds of hell to adopt your black babies truly woe be unto the lots of you because your hell will be worse than theirs. Thus saith the Lord thy God meaning it is so.</u>

Michelle and Michelle Jean

The lots of you do not realize that death wants every member in the black race to bow and submit to him.

Why do you think this is?

Loyalty!

Death has and have proven that humans – well blacks are not loyal; they will sell you out for the right price and death isn't wrong in this.

Look at how many go to Obeah Man and Woman to trample their own down.

Look how many participate in death rituals. Say it because all I have to do is point at the churches of death globally. This includes groups you join to get ahead in life by sacrificing humans and animals literally. **(Abrahamic Order of Death)**

We (not all) are loyal to death and not life; life too hard and long. You have to wait for success. All when yu a wait di devil an im people dem mek yu suffa.

Yes I am a living breathing testament of this. Death's children make it so hard for you that you give up. Look how many times I've given up. But I keep going no matter how mi gi up.

MY MANY QUESTIONS TO GOD

If Good God truly loves you, he will not let you give up. You must and will persevere over all the wickedness Satan's children throw your way.

Obeah and Voodoo is of the devil hence when evil tie yu, truly good luck because of sanity. Yu life tun dung and it's truly not easy for you to break this tie and rise again.

Truss mi dem want yu fi guh mad wussa dan catus cat.

Dem want yu fi guh neakid pan or inna di street.

Yu fi nayam outta garbage can because dem set yu suh. Trust me I know the wickedness of evil. I know the ties of evil because when yu tie you cannot break this tie. You have to go through it if you are ordained to. This is why some go mad – insane literally.

Think it doesn't happen to me? Read these books and see. Evil and the hosts of hell do not want you to succeed, so they do all for you to fail and yes go freaking insane.

Do I know why this has to truly be?

No.

Is this fair to you?

No because what you go through you do not want or need others to go through it. Hence I plead with Good God for truth and a saving grace for all the good and true seeds he's given me.

I need better for all his children and people. Evil should not hinder anyone from the good they want and need to do.

Evil should not hinder anyone from knowing the full truth. Hence it is my true will that Good God shuts down these Obeah Men and Women, Voodoo Priest and Priestesses including Shaman and Soothsayers. Life isn't about death it's about good and true life; hence all that is wicked and evil must be shut down more than infinitely and indefinitely more than forever ever without end.

No one should live in hate and lies. Come on now.
So if I am ordained to do so, I will more than infinitely and indefinitely write the punishment of these people and present my case to Good God and the Universe.

Michelle
March 15, 2015

Good God and Allelujah, Lovey what am I missing with you?

Lovey I saw this beautiful Air Canada plane flying over head but yet I was not on it. So why am I missing my flight and flights with you?

What am I doing wrong that I have to be grounded and cannot fly?

Yes the plane was coming in to land. It was a connecting flight, so why am I not connecting; on this connecting flight with you?

Yes the houses on the ground were beautiful and plenty, the trees around it was green and beautiful hence the beauty of you on earth and in flight. But why am I with this Babylonian man?

What does Babylonian men have to do with me?

I keep seeing Babylonian Men more and more and I truly cannot comprehend this. Why are they around me smiling?

It's as if they are protecting me but yet you know how I feel about Babylonians; the lie that they tell. Well this is humans on a whole and I cannot generalize anymore. Yes this is prejudicial on my part but what am I truly missing with you because I truly don't know?

I am so confused right now. So please unconfuse me because I truly don't know what to do.

I know where you want me to be. I see the beauty of this place and I will not stray from it. I will not stray from the Cayman Islands because I know you need a home there. So yes the Cayman will be for me and you. So yes the tree planting will now begin because I need to more than beautify this place. I have to truly make it good and clean; truthful and more than clean for me and you. And yes the island must be debt free, financially, spiritually, physically and emotionally including cleanliness wise. No Obeah and Voodoo bullshit must they do.

So to the people of Cayman, Good God need a home in you so please whatever evils that you do, let's put a stoppage to it so that Good God can truly come home to you.

Your land is his vacation home away from home so let's truly keep the Cayman Islands clean. You now know what he Good God and Allelujah want and need, so truly do not lose him like my people in

Jamaica did. We lost him including his name and now He's coming to you so truly give him a home.

<u>Bless up yourself because truth must now come out of you. So if you are doing illegal things financially, emotionally, spiritually please stop and clean up your land. He wants to bless you truthfully so truly listen.</u>

Listen the Cayman Islands is not the only land that is being called. Russia is being called and I truly don't know why because I am confused right now. I truly don't know what I am missing because I can't figure out anymore. I am weak right now because my body is being drained whist writing this book. I know death comes and I cannot stop this death because it was ordained so. So truly keep your island clean so that you can pass over death when it comes. Meaning your island will not be destroyed like Jamaica.

Destruction must come and take all who are wicked and evil because they live for evil; do all that is wicked and evil.

So as I interrupt the flow of this book truly listen and clean up the Cayman Island because Good God and Allelujah is looking towards you. You have a saving grace in him so hold on to your victory and forever ever come clean. Do not stray from goodness and cleanliness; truth. He is giving you something that a lot of our forefathers rejected. Please do not reject him. Accept him and do all that is good and clean; true. **Truth is everlasting life so truly live truthful in all that you do.**

Yes death must take their wicked and evil people everywhere. If you are good continue doing good because goodness and truth is your saving grace in all of this. Truth is everlasting life so live truthfully in all that you do. If you are doing bad things slowly turn from the bad that you do. Ask for forgiveness of those you have wronged and live.

Michelle and Michelle Jean

Good God if this is the message you want me to give to the people of the Cayman Island let it be delivered in goodness and in truth because I truly do not know what I am missing with you.

Like I said, I refuse to spread hate nor will I hate anyone based on hue and or whatever bullshit society hate on. I also refuse to hate you for the lies you tell because hating you does not become me. There's an app for hate and that app is hell. You want to hate and destroy go right ahead. Yes we all have a right to hate and loathe, I do at times but I do not dwell on these things nor do I let them consume me. Hence I leave hatred in hell and move on with my life the best I can. I refuse to pick up arms against you because my words of truth are my weapon and weapons. Plus I know how to cuss reckless and rude because mi a raw baane Jamaican and the one thing wi noa fi du a cuss yu good and proper. Many of us do not take bullshit hence many of us are not liked. You chose lies and hate then leave earth with your bullshit. Go to hell with death hence death must take you out of the presence of earth because "THE WAGES OF SIN IS DEATH" AND DEATH MUST INFINITELY AND INDEFINITELY UPHOLD THIS LAW. We cannot change this anymore Good God. We can no longer interfere with this law and I've told you this already. We cannot save people that willingly give themselves over to death. You've tried time and time again and have failed and the failure stops. **_The black race have and has proven to you time and time again that THEY STAND WITH DEATH AGAINST YOU; hence you must leave them alone to the choice and choices they've made._**

Lovey I can't keep missing your plane. I am fed up of this hence we have to come clean and communicate properly. Leave wicked and evil people alone. But as for me, I need to be secure in you more than indefinitely. My security in you and with you must be that impenetrable. Remember my cousin called me and told me about my sister and his wife in blue. To give you an abbreviated version of his conversation with me; he said he tried praying for me and this man, bronze man was blocking him; his prayer. His prayer could not come through because this man was blocking him. He could not penetrate this man. He said he could not see the man's face. Hence I told you no dirty person can pray for me. I am set with you hence all must be impenetrable when it comes to wicked and evil people in regards to me and you. I truly love you hence no Muslim or Islamist or Christian that live for death must penetrate us in all that they do; try.

My love of truth for you is pure; more than solid and I need this to stay with us more than infinitely and indefinitely forever ever without end. I cannot afford to lose you and my truth of you because of anyone. So truly stop letting me miss my flights with you. You are more than precious to me and I more than cherish the little time we have with each other.

We as humans and people have to clean up ourselves. Like I've said in some of the other books in the Michelle Jean series of books, **YOU DO NOT LOCK ANYONE OUT OF YOUR KINGDOM AND OR ABODE, WE AS HUMANS LOCK OURSELVES OUT WITH OUR SINS.**

I will not change this because WE ALL BELONG. WE ARE THE ONES THAT LET OTHERS TELL US WE DO NOT BELONG.

Yes I can say someone do not belong. You've shown me who belong to you and who does not in this day and time and this is due to sin; the wrongs we do on a daily basis. **Some can change the outcome of their lives but billions cannot because they accepted death in the living.** Yes this is sad and I will not change this because this was their good and true choice. And it matters not if they were deceived. We've all been deceived but some has and have learnt from this deceit. I did and I am still learning until this day. There's many things to learn and I truly need to learn them but I need to learn them from you. Yes I know

MY MANY QUESTIONS TO GOD

there is music there, advice from others, movies and so forth and this is great, but with me missing your flight constantly; I cannot live with this anymore. I don't want to continue to miss you. Maybe you're telling me I miss you too much in thought and reality.

Maybe this is your way of telling me that you miss me and you're coming home to me. Lovey, that Air Canada plane was beautiful. I've never seen such a beautiful plane before. It was small and compact, a bit chubby but truly beautiful. Wow. You are gorgeous, more than gorgeous and if this is truly you then honey I don't want to ever lose you.

So we both miss each other but we are coming home. I do see you and your beauty and I truly miss you too because I know the different levels of you.

So no, I will not stray from the Cayman Islands because I know you want me to be there. I know you need your vacation home there and I will do my best to get you this home.

So truly guide me to the right avenues that I must go in order to get you your home.

And Good God I truly miss her, my mother on this day. As this is the anniversary of her death my heart goes out to her. Please continue to save her and make her safe with you. I miss her too hence I have to go visit her grave soon. I have to bring her flowers like I use to. Thank you Lovey for reminding me of her because I truly love her too. Thank you both for truly being there for me. I more than unconditionally and truly love you both truthfully. You are both my world and earth and I praise you both because you are both true to me. True and pure love always.

I also know that some Muslims have a saving grace in the grave. Those that joined Islam and truly did not know that it is spiritual hell. I know you made provisions for them and I give you my word of truth and honour; integrity that I will not take this provision from them even though I've condemned Islam. They too need hope and a chance to be saved. So as I remember my mother in truth, I truly save her and take her soul and spirit out of the land of hell. Let her spirit and body including bones truly rest with you because I truly and duly wholeheartedly save her and you.

Michelle and Michelle Jean
March 12 and 15, 2015

Back on Board

Good God truly separate your people from the rest of the world as I think of the Islamic agenda. You know once this happens there will be no peace on earth because slavery will be on earth more than ten folds. Egypt was a testament, no more than a testament of the brutality our ancestors faced. The slavery in the west (AMERICAS) is and was more than a testament of what our ancestors faced. And I will not stop talking about how black babies were fed to alligators IN THE UNITED STATES OF AMERICA Good God and you permit this to happen. Hence you can only love us so and not true. <u>So the brutality that is to come I will close my eyes to it because as BLACK PEOPLE WE DO NOT LEARN. WE WOULD RATHER DIE WITH DEATH RATHER THAN WALK AWAY FROM IT.</u> SO IT MATTERS NOT WHAT HAPPENS TO BLACK PEOPLE TO ME ANYMORE BECAUSE WE ARE TOO DAMNED STUBBORN AND STIFF NECKED. SOMEONE AND SOMETHING IS HURTING US AND INSTEAD OF WALKING AWAY, WE STAY IN IT. I want to walk away from you Good God because you are stubborn also. You don't listen to good council so when people leave your ass you too should not complain because in truth you allow shit to happen to us. In a way and to me you use as sacrifices unto death. YOU WILLINGLY PERMIT THE SACRIFICE OF US IN ALL THAT YOU DO, SO HOW RIGHT ARE YOU. Yes this is the way I feel on this day hence I am interrupting the flow of this book yet again. I have to tell you all because the treatment of your true people is more than appalling. Why should any of us live in sin because of you?

Why should any of us be indebted to sin because of you?

You want cleanliness and truth but yet YOU ARE SACRIFICING US TO LIES AND DECEIT; DEATH and this is truly not fair.

How the hell can you say you love us so and watch us die?

You leave us hopeless and helpless in all that we do. This is more than bullshit on your part. This is hatred. You can't want us to be with you and continue to let us wallow in shit with wicked and evil people. It was never this way before so what changed you?

Did you give in to evil and become weak as evil?

Did you give up like I want to give up on you on many days?

Look at what my cousin said about the man in bronze protecting me. He (the bronze man) would not let his prayer go through, so why are you not more than defending your true people in this way?

Why are you allowing sin and evil, wicked and evil people get to us?

Where is your care and truth of us and for us?

LOVEY, I AM CONFUSED BECAUSE I KEEP DREAMING ABOUT LOS ANGELES AND I TRULY DO NOT KNOW WHAT YOU WANT ME TO DO.

YOUR PEOPLE RESIDE THERE BUT HOW DO I HELP THEM TO GET OUT OF BABYLON BEFORE IT'S TOO LATE. I FAILED WHEN I WAS THERE REMEMBER. RIGHT NOW I TRULY DON'T KNOW WHERE TO TURN. REMEMBER ROMMEL TOLD ME SHE TIED ME. SHE'S DEAD GOOD GOD AND HE'S DEAD, SO TRULY RELEASE ME BECAUSE THEY FAILED IN ALL THAT THEY TRIED IN THEIR WICKEDNESS TOWARDS ME. I NEED YOU SO TRULY LET THE WICKEDNESS BE TRULY DONE WHEN IT COMES TO ME. STOP LETTING WICKED AND EVIL PEOPLE TIE ME. FREE ME SO THAT I CAN LIVE. I NEED TO DO GOOD BECAUSE GOODNESS IS IN ME TO DO AND UNDER NO CIRCUMSTANCES SHOULD YOU ALLOW WICKED AND EVIL PEOPLE AND SPIRITS TO HURT ME. YES I HAD TO GO THROW THIS TO PROVE A POINT TO EVIL AND THEIR PEOPLE, BUT LOOK AT THE COST TO ME AND YOU GOOD GOD. TRULY LOOK AT THE COST BECAUSE I'VE DOUBTED YOU, CAST DOUBT ON YOU, CUSSED YOU RUDE. YES I MADE YOU MY ALL BUT DOES THAT MAKE IT ANY BETTER TO LASH OUT AT THE ONE YOU TRULY LOVE LIKE THIS BECAUSE OF PAIN AND HURT. NO ONE SHOULD HAVE TO DO THIS TO YOU. YES YOU WERE THERE WITH ME BECAUSE YOU MORE THAN TOOK MY STORMS OF BRUTAL CUSSING AND PUNISHMENT. HENCE I KNOW

THAT YOUR ANGER AND TEMPERMENT IS NOT AS FIERCE AND BRUTAL AS MINE. SO PLEASE LET THE BATTLE BETWEEN FATHER AND DAUGHTER, ME AND YOU STOP MORE THAN INFINITELY AND INDEFINITELY FOREVER EVER WITHOUT END INDEFINITELY. <u>I NEED TRUTH AND WHEREVER I CAN RIGHT THE WRONG THAT WAS DONE TO YOU, TRULY LET IT BE DONE. BUT IN ALL THAT I DO AND YOU DO, KNOW THAT I WILL STAND AGAINST YOU WHEN IT COMES TO WICKED AND EVIL PEOPLE AND SPIRITS THAT USE OBEAH AND VOODOO; ALL MANNER OF NEGATIVE ENERGY TO HURT PEOPLE IF YOU EVER GIVE THEM THESE WICKED AND EVIL DEMONS A WAY INTO YOUR KINGDOM AND ABODE.</u> NEVER EVER UNDER ANY CIRCUMSTANCES LOOK TO ME TO FAVOUR YOU. I WILL WALK AWAY FROM YOU IF YOU LET THESE WICKED AND EVIL DEMONS THAT WILLINGLY USE VOODOO AND OBEAH; ALL SHORTS OF EVIL TO HURT PEOPLE LIKE THEY'VE DONE ME A WAY IN. CONSIDER US OVER FROM NOW IF YOU CONTINUE TO LET THIS NASTY PRACTICE HAPPEN GLOBALLY. IT HURTS GOOD GOD HENCE TRULY LOOK AT MY PAIN AND HURT AND HOW I LASHED OUT AT YOU. I WANTED YOU TO KILL ME; DIE BECAUSE OF THIS. NO ONE SHOULD HAVE TO GO THROUGH THIS BECAUSE THEY TRULY LOVE YOU MORE THAN UNCONDITIONALLY COME ON NOW. HE HURT ME, SHE HURT ME HENCE I WILL NEVER GIVE ANY FORGIVENESS TO THEM NOR WILL I EXTEND THE OLIVE BRANCH TO ANYONE THAT WORK INIQUITY COME ON NOW. I MORE THAN INFINITELY AND INDEFINITELY FOREVER EVER WITH OUT END LOCK THESE PEOPLE (OBEAH MAN AND WOMAN, VOODOO

PRIEST AND PRIESTESSES, SHAMANS, SATANIST AND THE LIKES OF THEM THAT IS WICKED AND EVIL) OUT OF YOUR KINGDOM AND WORLDS GOOD GOD MORE THAN UNCONDITIONALLY. NO WAY IN MUST THEY HAVE COME ON NOW. YOU ARE MY RIGHT BUT YOU ARE WILLING TO ALLOW THESE NASTY PEOPLE TO TAKE ME FROM YOU. THEN YOU DON'T WANT OR NEED TRUTH AND TRUE LOVE. AND DON'T YOU DARE SAY HOW DARE YOU BECAUSE I KNOW YOU. And don't you dare tell me that I have no right to do this; lock these people out of your kingdom and abode. AND I AM TELLING YOU WHEN YOU PUT YOUR RING ON MY FINGER, GAVE ME YOUR LAST NAME, MADE ME YOUR TRUE DAUGHTER, GAVE ME THE RIGHT TO STOP DEATH (see Jamaica and Haiti), TOLD ME TO WRITE YOU A BOOK NOT ONCE BUT TWICE, WHEN YOU'RE IN THE STORM AND STORMS OF DEATH WITH ME THEN I HAVE ALL RIGHT TO EXERCISE MY RIGHT AND RIGHTS WITH YOU WHEN IT COMES TO DEATH AND THEIR WICKED AND EVIL PEOPLE. MY UNCONDITIONAL LOVE OF TRUTH AND PERFECTION WHEN IT COMES TO YOU ALSO GAVE ME THAT RIGHT. REMEMBER YOU GAVE ME SEEDS TO PLANT OVER 100 MILLION ACRES AND YOU ALSO TOLD ME YOU WANT A 25 MILLION DOLLAR MEGA MANSION. SO IF ALL THIS DOES NOT SPEAK VOLUMES WHEN IT COMES TO ME AND YOU AND MY RIGHT AND RIGHTS OF YOU THAN SOMETHING IS TRULY WRONG. YOU ARE MINE AND WHAT I TRULY LOVE I DO TAKE CARE OF AND WILL DEFEND FIERCELY IN ALL THAT I DO. SO TRULY DON'T GO THERE BECAUSE YOU ARE TRULY MINE; MY UNCONDITIONAL RIGHT AND RIGHTS.

NO ONE SHOULD HAVE TO GO THROUGH EVIL TO GET TO YOU. YOU ARE NOT EVIL YOU ARE TRUTH AND THE TRUTH CANNOT HURT. THE TRUTH IS LIFE AND LIFE DO NOT HURT, WICKED AND EVIL PEOPLE HURT.

WICKED AND EVIL PEOPLE DO ALL TO STOP THE TRUTH AND THIS SHOULD NOT BE. WICKED AND EVIL PEOPLE DO NOT WANT TO RELIQUISH POWER AND THIS SHOULD NOT BE. NO WICKED AND EVIL PERSON AND OR NATION AND OR GOVERNMENT SHOULD HAVE CONTROL OVER ANYONE COME ON NOW.

WHAT ARE YOU TELLING ME GOOD GOD? ARE YOU TELLING ME EVIL HAS CONTROL AND DOMINANCE OVER YOU? DON'T GO THERE BECAUSE I KNOW EVIL HATH TIME AND THE TIME OF EVIL IS UP; NOW THE HARVEST AND THE GATHERING MUST BEGIN, BUT I AM HURT AND I HAVE TO COME TO YOU. DEAR GOD MY BROTHER AND HIS CHILD IS IN THE BELLY OF THE BEAST AND I TRULY DO NOT KNOW HOW TO SAVE THEM. YES I CAN GO INTO THE BELLY OF THE BEAST AND TAKE HIM OUT BUT I CAN'T TAKE HIS CHILD BECAUSE OF HER. I WILL NOT SAVE HER BECAUSE THERE IS NO TRUE CONNECTION THERE AND THIS HURTS AND SADDENS ME. I CANNOT SAVE SOMEONE THAT I TRULY DO NOT CARE ABOUT OR HAVE A CONNECTION WITH. MY BROTHER I TRULY LOVE BECAUSE HE'S ALWAYS BEEN THERE FOR ME SO I HAVE TO DO ALL TO SAVE HIM BECAUSE HE'S A PART OF MY LOVE OF TRUTH AND TRUE LOVE. GOOD GOD I AM HURTING BECAUSE I FEEL HELPLESS AND YOU ARE NOT

OPENING TRUE AND GOOD DOORS FOR ME. PLEASE TELL ME WHAT TO DO BECAUSE I KNOW THE DEATH THAT IS COMING AND I CAN'T SAVE THEM. WHY?

WHY CAN'T WE CHANGE THIS GOOD GOD BECAUSE MY BROTHER HAS AND HAVE BEEN GOOD TO ME. PLEASE GOOD GOD LET THEM FIND A WAY OUT BEFORE CALIFORNIA GOES UNDER THE SEA. *Dear God I need you. I can't take this helplessness anymore. How do I truly save my brother and his son? How do I help them to escape the judgment that's to come? I truly don't want to save her but I have to save her son. But yet I truly don't know how to. Good God and Allelujah truly save me and them. I am pleading to you because I truly don't know what to do.*

<u>Dear God you have to prepare your children and people to leave out of Babylonian lands right away.</u>

Give us the power to defeat the devil and his people Good God. Truly give us the power to defeat the devil and his people because I've made no provisions for any of them in our new kingdom and kingdoms of true peace and harmony; truth and tranquility; true love and true and good; positive life.

Lovey, we need your tools of survival right now because the devil's children are fired up to take lives on a massive scale. So in all that we do, we have to protect our own and leave the devil's children alone.

MY MANY QUESTIONS TO GOD

Have mercy Lovey because I am counting on you to secure our good and true people. I am counting on you to save my brother and his son.

Open his ears and let him listen Good God. Please do not fail me when it comes to them because like I've said, my brother has helped me. He's done a lot for me and I have to save him. I have to do all for him to save him before it's too late.

Lovey, please help me. I am pleading with you for goodness and a helping hand. Please do not let the devil use him and his child as a sacrifice. Please save him for me because of goodness no matter the tears I've shed because of him. He's never failed me so please do not let me fail him. Feel my pain and hurt if anything happened to him. Lovey, truly hear me and if I have any goodness on my record of truth that can save him as well let it truly be done; save him. Remember when I had no food he sent me money to buy food to feed my family. He gave me money to buy a sofa when we had none. He did try to help me with my health, so please I beg of you and humble myself to you and ask that you give my brother and his son a saving grace. Please do not let hell take them lest I be truly hurt; die.

Michelle and Michelle Jean, March 07 and 16, 2015

You know what Good God no one likes to be hurt. I certainly don't. I've come to realize the hard way that people hurt.

We hurt each other
Say things we do not mean
Can't live up to our promises; word.

For most of my life I've come to accept this. Accept the hurt of others including you and I refuse to anymore.

I refuse to let you and others hurt me.

Do not give me empty promises and false hope.

Do not lie to me in any way.

Things happen in life yes but me?

Why hurt me?

Why give when I cannot receive?
Why give when you are not truthful in your giving?
Why give when you know you cannot encourage?

Why give when you know you cannot be there for the person? Why give at all when you of yourself are not truthful, you are a liar and deceiver? s2

Why say you love so when loving so have no value; care?

Why love us so when loving us so cannot heal my sickness and pain including loneliness and broken heart?

Why love so if I am constantly telling you about truth and true love; my hurt and pain?

Why love so if I am constantly hurting; yearning?

Why say you love us so and leave us to die at the hands of death's children?

Why say you love us so and let death's children dominate and control society globally?

Why say you love us so when you truly don't give a damn. Your people including me have to beg you for good and true life; truth?

Your people have to bug you to separate them from evil; all evil and not even that you can do.

My devotion and truth is real; you. So why can't you be devoted and true to me in all that you do?

Why do I have to constantly be missing you?

Hence I will not allow you to hurt me anymore because your loving us so in not real. It's fake; false hope and I will not give humanity false hope because of you. Pain is real and you of yourself know this.

I also refuse to spread hate to please you. You are not me. You can hate, but I refuse to because WE ALL HAVE A RIGHT TO CHOOSE OUR OWN DESTINY AND BIILIONS DID. THEY DID NOT CHOOSE YOU AND YOU HAVE TO LIVE WITH THIS.

THIS IS YOUR REALITY GET USED TO IT.

Learn and know that true love is not false. It is real and pure and it's not everyone that can love true; pure. Hence true love is more than extremely rare.

Many cannot handle true love hence they live in lies and live for false hope; love and I cannot do this. My truth and true love have to be real and true. I refuse to accept anything else. So yes, I refuse loving so because loving so is truly not true in my book. Yes loving so is huge, a lot in your book but loving us so is not good enough in my book. I give true love hence I expect nothing less because true love heal, grow, flourish and goes up to you hence you have to be true and real to me in all that you do.

Like I said, true love is real, but yet to me you don't want it; true love. You can't handle it hence you run from me instead of truly embracing me.

Why is that?

Truth is everlasting life and if the God we serve and or look up to cannot truly love then what good are you to us?

Do not leave your true people in pain. Save them and let them grow and flourish with you.

Look at me and the way I am with you. If I could give you worlds and universes void of all sin and evil I would.

If I could sing or even hum a love song to you just to make you feel special; good, I would without hesitation.

Yes I piss you off, but Good God, who haven't I pissed off? I need your attention on some days and when I don't get it, I do something to piss you off. **Did I not also tell you in my way that I wanted to go to St.**

Petersburg, Russia and stay at the Belmond Grand Hotel Europe in the Presidential suite just to see if they toss the furniture and linen out when I left? Yes I would piss off people because I wanted to see just how racist they were when it comes to black people.

Yes this is cheeky on my part but hey, my mind do think crazy things at times. But to piss off someone because I was staying at the Belmond Grand Hotel in St. Petersburg Russia would be icing on the cake for me in a cheeky kind of way. *(Racism. Yes I want to see just how racist Russians can be when it comes to hue.)*

I know don't start nothing but I truly want to do this. Or just have about fifty or more black people staying at the hotel at the same time us just to piss someone off. And people please do not ask me why I want to do this, but my spirit wants to. Hence I tell you everything and you know it.

<u>Yes people this is wickedness on my part but I truly don't know why my spirit wants to piss these people off in this way.</u>

Michelle

Do good unto others and good will follow you. So why aren't you following me and your people Good God?

Look at the earth and see what the demon seeds of the world is doing.

Gun violence, beheadings, murder, rape have escalated and this is what you want your people to live in and see?

Tell me something Good God, is this some kind of sick joke on your part?

Many build bombs and ammunition to kill and have killed and you're okay with this bullshit?

Now tell me yet again, when did you become Aries the God of War?

When did you become death?

When did the ills of man become loving us so by you?

Was she right and or correct when she said God kills? Was she?

Is my loving you true in vain?
Is my true devotion to you in vain?
Are you even capable of true love?

So tell me now, why am I questioning your integrity? Yes I am hurt on this day because I am tired of being hurt by you and others.

I am tired of making excuses for you.
I am tired of living in your lonely shadow; life.

What good is a man if they are constantly living in fear; pain?

Why should I fear or live in fear of losing you?

This is wrong. So is devoting to someone your truth when they are not deserving of it.

Do not give false hope because I refuse to hate anyone for you. Death shows us his world and we know what death can do. You on the other hand do not. We have nothing to live for and don't you dare say you have me. You've provided for us. Yes grant you this. But in truth do you truly provide for us?

Emotionally where are you in that department when it comes to our true happiness.

You know how I am when it comes to happiness and cleanliness. So why are you not loving true and not just so?

Michelle and Michelle Jean

Yes I am down on you this morning Good God and rightfully so. I've set myself up for failure because man fail all around and I am so no exception to the rule. Hence I have to clam up again and truly go back to my reclusive life.

I also have to shut you out because of hurt and pain. I am tired of being hurt by humans; tired of living by false hope and lies.

I have to do me because I am not getting any younger, I am getting older. I want to say I cannot rely on you anymore but I can't. Right now I have to choose a better way and life for me.

I am tired of talking and complaining to you and you're not listening to me. Hence I do comprehend why so many have and has walked away from you.

I fully comprehend why billions say there is no God as well as say no to you.

Lovey, we are confused and lost and no matter how we try to find you, we cannot. Yes look within but look within where?

Where inside do we look to find you?
We have no instruction manual.

We have no button to push. Hence you cannot keep us in the dark. We need to find you because there's a great energy there that man knows nothing about.

You cannot be our false hope come on now.

Right now I want to run away from all including you. I need a stable relationship with you not one that fluctuates and is based on hurt and pain.

I did not choose this road for me; the road of hurt and pain. So why do you continue to keep me on it; this hurtful and painful road?

Where and when does stability come in?

Lovey, why should I or anyone feel bipolar and depressed with you?

Why drive us insane in this way? Confusion is a bitch, so why do you confuse and keep us confused?

Yes I hate and or loathe these days of uncertainty because no one should have to live uncertain if you gave them true life.

Michelle and Michelle Jean

An uncertain life with you Good God is truly not what I want or need.

I do not want or need a god that cannot truly love.

I do not need a god that cannot help me to be more emotionally stable with him her; both.

I do not need a god that truly cannot provide for me emotionally, financially, health wise, truth wise, honesty wise, clean wise, good all around.

I need balance; true balance in my life Good God and you cannot balance me because I keep complaining. I complain a lot and this shouldn't be.

Now tell me at what point in the relationship does stability come in?

At what point in the relationship do I say fuck it, I am gone? I can't be devoted and true to someone that can only love so. Yes loving us so is a lot but I want and need truth not so.

True love is cleaner in my book and it's obvious we are not from the same book nor are we on the same page. Am I cussing you out this morning? No, just voicing my concerns due to my hurt and pain.

MY MANY QUESTIONS TO GOD

Do I hate being disappointed by others?

Yes and yes welcome to your world when it comes to us and humans hurting you.

Yes I know the pain hence we need to be truly balanced emotionally and in all that we do.

Lovey, we need balance. I'm unbalanced hence I tip over. Have tipped over time and time again when it comes to you and this is wrong. We truly need stability; balance. Yes a truly balanced balance sheet.

Lovey, we need to live but we need to live true. Hence truly look at this earth because I need a world and home with you that is totally balanced, clean, good, prosperous, healthy, wise, more than good and positive all around. Yes I know the house for me but Lovey, where's the mountains and the hills that I can walk up. Why flat lands when you know I truly don't like flat. I have to have my mountains and hills to look at; go up and down on. Walk up and down to get my blood and heart circulating.

You know me so truly provide for me.

Michelle and Michelle Jean

MY MANY QUESTIONS TO GOD

Yes early this morning I took out my frustrations on you Good God. I truly thank you for listening to me and being my beating stick once again.

Like I said, I need our relationship to be truly solid, meaning I need stability in my emotions when it comes to you.

You are special to me hence you are my good listener and true friend. Yes I know you rarely talk but regardless of that you do make me find my way.

So truly thank you for all that you do for me. Hopefully soon I can bloat your head and boost you my way.

So as I kick it old school truly listen to Save the World by Peetah Morgan and Fullfilment Time by Tony Tuff and Smokie Benz.

Listen to what Peetah said about corruption.

Truly hear this song Good God because it is going to get brutal real soon. You cannot let Babylon rise again ever over man.

Death lost, so Islam and all facets of religion must go down with him.

Lovey, squash the Islamic Agenda – All Religious Agenda because I refuse to go down with them. I refuse to let your children and people go down to hell with them; death's demonic people and children.

People kill for death; a place in hell so truly let wicked and evil people go. Good including you have to know that the devil cannot be reformed. Evil is evil hence evil will always kill; do evil to maintain their place in hell and this is truly sad.

Yes death is a god and death kills but this can no longer be Good God. I refuse to share you and my world which is our world with evil; wicked and evil people and spirits.

Lovey we were given choices and billions chose death over you so let them be. Let the gods of humanities choosing now save them.

You cannot continue to uphold slackness and I've told you this. You are not a religion hence leave humanity to the evil choice they make; but truly save me and your good and true people including you.

Michelle and Michelle Jean

Hear what Peetah said about corrupt systems in Save the World. **He said it's the "CHOICE" we've been making.** He is correct. We as humans vote these corrupt politicians into office.

We as humans buy into their lies. So yes we are to be truly blamed for the evils they inflict upon us.

Did Eve (Evening) not do the same bullshit with the Babylonian that we call Satan?

Did Ethiopia not do the same thing by disrespecting you and siding with the devil and his people against you?

Did Egypt not fall for the same bullshit hence the brutal slaveries of old?

Did Judah (Jamaica) not do the same bullshit?
Did we not keep the order of death for the Israelites (Ethiopia)? See the hair on the heads of all Rasta's globally. Hence I tell them not to cut their hair. This hair is our reminder of the death angel that yanks your spirit from the body before your body goes back to the earth to be eaten by worms, thus leaving only your bones.

Did he not try the same bullshit with me and I rejected him?

I do not need dirty money Good God. I need clean money; your money and lands.

I need a clean home void of filth; sin and evil. So why would I accept him?

He offers me nothing because at the end of the day all that he's given to me will be taken away. I have to leave it behind. I have to face death because I am indebted to him and my children and family will be also.

Death is not my choice; good and clean life is. I need true peace Lovey. I need an environment that's clean and prosperous. I need my waters of life to be clean and pure.

I need my food and mate to be organic not inorganic.

Look at society today Good God, strung up on vanity. No one wants to grow old gracefully why?

Dear God look, truly look at what humanity call beauty. None is as beautiful as nature and none is as clean and pure as the waters of earth. This is why they pollute all. They want all to become dirty and unclean as them. Pity because shortly humanity will have to reap the fruits of their sorrows; labour.

So Lovey truly see. And when this all goes down ensure our good and true people are in the lands they need to be. Please ensure they have plenty of clean water and food to last them for more than infinite and indefinite lifetimes and generations more than infinitely and indefinitely forever ever without end.

I'm a foodie Lovey and you know this, so never ever let any starvation come to us. We must plant what we need and eat what we need. We must also help our good and true lands <u>*only*</u>. The devil's people and children we must know them not and help them not.

Good God you can continue to help them but not me. I truly know the hurt and pain of evil hence I have to stay away from all that is wicked and evil.

You know I am not as generous as you when it comes to wicked and evil people and spirits.

My heart is clean and good but because of pain and hurt I cannot have this good and clean heart for people who constantly hurt others.

Why should someone grieve because of his and her wickedness and that evil and wicked person go free?

Come on now tell me where there is fairness in this?

I've made you my good and true choice including true devoted, so why should someone come along and take this from me?

Why should anyone put enmity and strife between us come on now?

Why can't I live good and true with you?

No Lovey, I truly can't live with this type of dissention and hate when it comes to me and you.

I need true life for me and my family including the good and true seeds you've given to me.

These seeds that I now plant that was given from you Good God and Allelujah must be good and true; clean and positive and never evil. These seeds must grow and have good and true, clean and positives fruits for more than infinite and indefinite lifetimes and generations forever ever without end. None absolutely none can or must have bad fruits come on now Good God.

No, I cannot have any be evil or bare bad fruits. I more than truly love you more than unconditionally so why would I ask you for bad fruits come on now?

Michelle and Michelle Jean

I'm sorry Lovey but I can't be as generous as you.

Someone don't like me, why should I have anything to do with them?

Lovey you long to me
You are my Jackfruit Tree
Mango Tree (Millie)
Breadfruit Tree
Yam
Banana
Dumpling
Bread
Cassava

Gungo Peas
Broad Beans
No not chick peas. Don't eat it.

You are my coffee
Morning Dew and I'm to share you with wicked and evil people? Yu nuh love mi true den?

Lovey yu noa how gungo peas soup nice and sweet. An mi fi gi dem a lickle bit a yu?

Noa sa naah goh happen.

You are my right and dem suh dutty and nasty.

No I refuse to clean dem up. Mek dem clean up self. On this day yu are mine and I am more than holding on tight without sharing. YES MI A NYAM OFF DI FOOD; YU.

LAADE AN GOOD GOD, THINK A DI DUMPLING; YU. Soup nuh nice without dumpling. Suh if mi ha fi mi dumpling inna mi soup wey mi a guh share it fa an mi done greedy fi yu aready?

Si, yu nuh fair. Yu gimme yu, yu neva sey share yu.

Nuh laugh.

Mi ha yu wey mi a share yu fa an eee tek so long fi get yu. Noa sa not in my book on this day.

All di mango and food a fi mi an mi guh cack up mi foot and nyam till mi belly full. Wey mi canne eat mi pudung till later then mi eat mi belly full again.

Yes it's greed on my part but then Good God it's you. So why shouldn't I be greedy for you? Hence I dedicate *TOUCH AND GO SITUATION* by Beres Hammond to you on this day.

Michelle and Michelle Jean

Good God whether you like this book or not it has to be written. You cannot say you love us so and give false hope.

Mother Africa is tired, the universe is tired and I'm tired also. I'm tire of the bloodshed and bloodletting.

Regardless of our evil choices Good God, Earth should not be left in ruin and decay by anyone including you.

Do not treat life like a game because it is not. Life is precious you and I know this, but if a man woman or child walk away from life and choose death, then truly leave them alone; let them go. Hence this song, WHERE WERE YOU by Beres Hammond YOU NEED TO DEDICATE TO ALL IN HUMANITY THAT DID NOT CHOOSE YOU. You are humanities circus clown that they can let go and run back to when things don't work out with the god and gods that they choose and this should not be. So yes this is an appropriate song for you to dedicate to them, hence I dedicate this song to them on your behalf.

Let death provide for them because death is their choice. Yes there are consequences to our actions but you have to leave these people alone and move on.

You cannot constantly extend the life line of your trees to humanity and they keep rejecting you. It can no longer work.

Listen to JUST SAY NO by Beres Hammond and listen because the people of the globe; your good and true people are not safe amongst wicked and evil people. Like I've said, good should not suffer for the bad nor should they be muzzled by wicked and evil people.

Death has his and her people right where they want them, what about you?

Where do you have your people?
Where do we fit in in the grand scheme of things?

<u>Where do we go from here? So truly listen to JUST SAY NO by Beres Hammand BECAUSE WAR COMES AND THE TEARS WILL FLOW WORSE THAN RIVERS.</u>

YOUR TRUE AND GOOD PEOPLE NEED YOUR RIGHT AND TRUE DIRECTION NOW. IF YOU

<u>DON'T GIVE IT TO US NOW WE ARE GOING TO GO DOWN AND DIE WITH EVIL AND THEIR WICKED AND EVIL CHILDREN. YOU CANNOT PERMIT THE SLAUGHTER OF YOUR PEOPLE LIKE THIS COME ON NOW.</u>

You are our hope and truth. We are living to be with you hence it is now time for us to be separated from all that is wicked and evil globally. You cannot let us fall with death and their children.

You cannot continue to let us live like the broken because we are truly not broke, we have you. You are our financial institutions.

You are our life, good life and balance sheet.

You are our global economy that grows in goodness and truth, so let us come home in life, goodness and truth to you come on now.

A nation and people that die without truth are dead. They cannot live by the truth nor

can they speak the truth. You know this Lovey but yet you refuse to live right and do right.

Lies are negatives, they cannot come right nor can they be clean or come clean. So truly think because life; true life does not sway this way and that way.

You cannot constantly let your good and true people live in fear.

You cannot continue to let them live wrong. This is wrong on your part. Yes I know the abundance of goodness you have towards all in humanity but there comes a point in time when you truly have to think and say what am I doing, this isn't right and truly walk away. You and I cannot live by a little hope. We will never progress and you see this with humanity when it comes to you. All you've given us we've tainted and destroyed. Look at your name and the way we abuse it.

Look at the sanctuaries we say we dedicate onto you. Death lives in them hence we bring our dead in them to be buried; sealed in hell for a time before the spirit eventually dies.

Man is the root of all evil because we do all manner of evil in thy sight.

We are truly not devoted to you. We cry to you for justice and as soon as justice comes we run to the houses of death and praise death for all you've done for us. So tell me how loyal are we to you?

I too want to leave you at times and yes many things I do, I want to piss you off because I'm restricted. But this is me. I am spoilt in many ways but it's unfortunate I can't have you my way all the time.

You as my true friend cannot wait on wicked and evil people to change.

And no you cannot shut me up either. I refuse to have you muzzle me because you need to hear the truth.

Evil cannot change and will never change, so truly leave wicked and evil people alone to their own demise. It's time for justice Good God and I keep telling you this. Evil failed in 2013 and it's now 2015 and you've done absolutely nothing to rid earth of the evil and evils that plague it.

Death wants his and her people, give it to them. No I will not cry for my homeland. I've told you the people dem too wicked and evil. You told me the land is unclean; dirty, so why would I want to save dirty people; wicked and evil people anymore. You gave us something good and instead of cherishing it, we made it unclean; dirty.

I've pissed off death enough hence she can have the people and the rivers of waters can cleanse the land.

Peace, true peace be unto the land of Jamaica but I will not stay the death of the wicked and evil people of the land. Nor will I stay the destruction and demise of Babylon and all her evil nations especially the United States of America. Young babies were fed to alligators. Black babies Good God, so no, their destruction stays because I've told you I will never forgive you for the mountains of LA and Nevada. Save your good and true people including my brother and son by giving them safe passage to another land.

None of your mountains should lay in decay and ruin because of man – humanity Good God. Mountains are significant to life because true life is found on mountains. You reside on mountains hence your children know the value of you and the significance of mountains. It's not everyone that can or will make it to the top. Been to the top and I did not like the top hence I chose the base of the mountain.

I will not relinquish the base of the mountain hence I have to plead with you for nature and the environment also. I need the waters of life hence judgment must come to all those who pollute the waterways constantly and on a daily basis.

I truly love the waters of Earth. They are our lifeline and we are to keep them clean all the time.

No Lovey, fair is fair. You cannot just think of humans – people that care nothing for you.

Humans can no longer destroy what you've given us. It's wrong.

As humans we cherish nothing and we value not life and this is truly sad. So why should you Good God value and cherish us? Why should you continuously extend a lifeline to us? Come on now.

Evil was unleashed on Earth Good God. Spiritual evil was stopped and now it's time to stop physical evil more than infinitely and indefinitely forever ever without end.

"The wages of sin is death" but "TRUTH IS EVERLASTING LIFE." Hence many on earth do not have truth and they cannot have eternal or everlasting life.

Humans did accept lies and not the truth Good God hence religion did spread to the four corners of the globe and destroy.

Religion is death you and I know this hence billions are slated to die before 2032.

Like I said, close the portals and doors to you after this because man is truly not deserving of you. You've tried but it's humans that failed you.

Billions have chosen the latter (Death) over you. Good and True Life – You were not the good and true choice of billions. So you truly have to let these people go and build a new again without evil.

Earth must become clean hence I ask of you yet again to take all that is wicked and evil out of me and from around me more than infinitely and indefinitely forever ever without end.

You are my more than good and true choice.

So let me be that girl that's the right one for you. _**Hence I dedicate THAT GIRL by Jah Cure to you.**_

So continue to hold on to me good and true because we still have a lot to do here on earth. Further, kiss my mother for me and tell her no matter what she is in my heart and I will do all to save her from the clutches of hell. I more than truly love her unconditionally. So Lovey in all that you do, truly remember my true love of her on this day, March 12.

It was on this day she joined you hence keep her truly save for me and cherish her like I cherish you.

True love can never die nor can it fade because it's true; the truth.

You are the truth also Good God hence TRUTH IS EVERLASTING LIFE.

Michelle

MY MANY QUESTIONS TO GOD

Good God why do we even bother?

Yes I am interrupting this book because black people truly get to me. I am getting angry at this very minute to see how foolish and ignorant we've become over the ages.

Our history was stolen from us.
Our history, no I should not use history, I should use life. Our life was stolen from us.

Our life has been tainted by a bunch of wannabee murderers that have robbed us of us including you.

They give us dirty religions of filth to keep us enslaved and unclean and we can't see this?

We can't see the shit that these people are doing is bringing us to hell with them.

We are sacrificing you Lovey for what?
We are sacrificing our lives and the lives of our family for what; a place in hell?

A piece of shit hole in hell whilst demons feed on the spirit and laugh.

Lovey when are we going to fucking wake up and see the truth of religion?

When are we going to stop being so fucking ignorant and know the truth about BLACK PRIDE AND LIVING; CLEANLINESS?

It gets to me that we cry to you for hope but yet still live as the fucking hopeless and downcast; down trodden.

People trample us down and we still take it. Have no ambition to rise up and say, fuck you and your whoring and deceitful systems. I don't have to take your bullshit; I am going back to the land and lands of my forefathers and mothers and I am going to build them positively. Kiss my ass I am out. Doublely fuck you because Africa is there for me. I am permanently out; you can find me on the beaches of Africa enjoying the sun and rain, dew and pleasures of my true and good people; my ancestors home.

Tell me Good God, where did black pride go?

Where did the ambition of the black race; true black race go?

Lovey I truly don't know because my spirit is pissed. Everyone has stolen from Black Life and we as a nation and race of people cannot learn and know this. So what's the point of you saving us if we cannot learn? We keep making the same mistakes over and over again.

MY MANY QUESTIONS TO GOD

Yes I know billions of blacks in hue do not belong to you but you cannot continue to neglect your true black own. Life, good and true life is given by you but from the way we are on earth and the sins we commit it does not seem so.

I am so pissed at THE GLOBAL BLACK RACE THAT I WANT TO KNOCK THEM IN THE HEAD FOR THEM GO GET SOME GOOD AND TRUE COMMON SENSE.

We claim to be but we are so fucking stupid that I want to scream. Where the hell did religion come from you bunch of morons and dumb fucks? What god do you have to look for when you as a race have him already?

Wake the fuck up and know your true history and heritage and stop living like the fucking dead of hell.

Coop pan some a unnu, tattooed out like some of the demons of hell and truly don't know it. Hence your fucking tattoos are

your mark of the beast. Your fucking bond and bondage in hell. Your body, skin belongs to earth not man. Your spirit is what belongs to you and the flesh is your physical prison; the prison of the spirit. If the majority of you were true Africans; blacks you would have known this. You wouldn't be wallowing in the shit; dung of the religions of the devil. Come on now.

<u>Man made shit of lies and deceit to enslave and capture souls just to feed them to death and you the black race globally was the fucking target.</u>

Religion is shit and bullshit. Hence Aries the God of War as denoted by the Ram – the Quran and or Koran; Ramquran and or Ramqoran. Thus the fucking warmongers of these global religions of lies and deceit. Religions that lets you sign your death warrant with death; hell.

Tell me Lovey, did we as a race and people not learn from those SELL OUT AND TURNCOAT ETHIOPIANS, the original Jews. Yes the Ethers that signed a pact with death long before the birth of Adam and Eve in the Illuminati Book of Death – man's so called holy bible.

No Lovey, I am so pissed that I want to scream and say you fucking Black Morons, Islam is spiritual death. Once you join this farce of a religion and faith and change your name, you've signed your death warrant because you are going straight to hell and burn. Forget fucking Satan because he's not death. No one is stronger than death in his and her domain. The demons of hell is more powerful than Satan because Satan's their bitch.

Lovey I am so sorry this morning but you know me when I am mad. As Blacks we talk about Africa and the fucking lots of them don't know the fucking truth. They don't truly know that NOT ALL BLACK PEOPLE CAME FROM AFRICA. Africa is the birthplace of life, WATER. Life, true life started with water and spread globally and or throughout the planet. Hence many blacks are without roots. They are empty shells that swing this way and that way at the drop of a needle; dime.

No wonder nations can use religion to catch them because we've lost our spirituality and vibration; cleanliness.

<u>You are there but it's time we stop looking for a fucking place to belong with dirty people and fucking scum juice and bags of religions.</u>

YOU'RE NOT A FUCKING RELIGION. YOU ARE GOOD AND TRUE LIFE, HENCE WE ARE TO LIVE CLEAN AND STOP SINNING. YOU STOP NO ONE FROM LIVING LIFE GOOD GOD COME ON NOW.

But as controlled freaks and fools, we let people destroy our lives with their religious bullshit. NO ONE CAN TAKE RELIGION TO YOU.

NO ONE, ABSOLUTELY NO ONE CAN SAY, LET ME IN I AM CHRISTIAN AND I DESERVE TO BE HERE.

ABSOLUTELY NO ONE CAN SAY, I AM MUSLIM LET ME IN I DESERVE TO BE HERE.

Trust me they will more than get the fuck you sign in their faces because none can cross over to life, your life Good God.

And yes I am letting my anger get the best of me and I am sorry, but I can't stand the black race acting so foolish and stupid for religion.

No religion is in your world but yet we cannot see this.

I can't take religion to you Lovey, no one can. WE ALL KNOW THAT TRUTH IS EVERLASTING LIFE AND WE HAVE TO COME TO YOU WITH TRUTH AND CLEANLINESS. WE HAVE TO BE TRUTHFUL AND CLEAN TO YOU.

<u>Why the hell would you accept anything other than the truth and cleanliness come on now?</u>

Ah Lovey, you are the truth and true way but yet we accept lies and think we can come to you with this bullshit. Billions are slated to die, are going to die because they followed death to their graves and this is a crying shame.

WE ARE TO CHOOSE GOOD AND CLEAN LIFE NOT DEATH.

WE ARE TO LIVE TRUTHFUL AND CLEAN BUT YET WE CANNOT DO THIS.

Like fools we are looking for someone to save us when we of ourselves can save us. All we have to do is give up death and breakaway from lies and deceit.

No it will not be easy.

You will fall time and time again but pick yourself up, ask for forgiveness and move on. If you have to pay a sin offering, pay your damned sin offering if you can pay and live.

Yes you've given humanity a saving grace Lovey but how many has and have accepted this saving grace?

And no you will not tell anyone to die for another person's sins. Your sins you committed, so why should anyone come and die to save you? You did wrong and I'm to lay my life down for you? Truly fuck you; my life is important to me and Good God.

You did wrong, accept your wrongs and amend them. I will not amend them for you because you know what you did was wrong; deceitful.

No one should have to die for you and no one will. You wanted to live in deceit and lies; so pay for your deceit and lies. Why the hell should I go to hell and burn for you?

What about my family?

What about MY TRUE LOVE AND GOOD FOOD; LOVEY AND GOOD GOD? He more than matters to me so why the fuck should I give him up for you?

You die to see death not life because good and true life cannot die, it can only grow, hence the upward and or upright triangle. As humans we are to live upright and just in all that we do come on now.

So yes, I am angry Lovey because life is winding down here on earth and the black race seem to be no further ahead that when we started; gave you up long ago.

Why are we not learning Lovey?

No come on now Lovey, why are we not learning? Our past lives (forefathers and or ancestors life) was hell and we are still going through hell. Death isn't working for us, so why the hell are we sticking to and holding on to death?

Why can't we eliminate and or bypass death and keep on the pathway of cleanliness and righteousness?

Lovey, you are our truth, so why are we acting like Eve and letting someone tell us lies about you?

Do we not belong to you?

Do we not know you?

So why give you up for the lies and death of other gods? Come on now.

I know the goodness in you and you treat me more than good. Why should I give this up to live like Eve?

Why should I accept pain and death when I can live pain free forever ever without end with you?

Lovey, hell is not pretty, meaning there is no water there only fire. I need water. Our spirit need water so why would I give up water for fire. Fire can't clean me it can only kill me.

Fire can't quench my thirst only water can, so why would I give up life for death?

Yes I know the spirit urges you to do wrong when you are stressed I know. Trust me if I could get rid of negative and or evil will just like that I would. I would not hesitate to do so, but unfortunately at this stage of my life I cannot but one day I will.

So My Darling and True Love, for all the sins humanity has and have done on earth and beyond for more than centuries, I more than infinitely and indefinitely forever ever give you **I SWEAR by All For One to you.** Yes I am going back old school but that's okay because if I could build you your true and solid home void of all sin and evil I will; would.

I know you asked me for a 25 million dollar mega mansion and I need to build you this home right away so that we can get away together from the pain and sins; sufferings of this world.

Ah Lovey, I am with you and if I could do all for you I would and will because you more than deserve it.

So keep being my good and true heart beat.
Keep being my good and true emotions and all.

You are worth it and you are a BIG DEAL. (Christopher Martin)

Big up yourself because one day, all your pain will go away and wicked and evil people will be no more. You will be free to walk the earth you created without hindrance from wicked and evil people and spirits.

Know that you are in my thoughts and although I get angry and swear; it is not a reflection on you. Remember I am a female Lyon (lion) and we are more than fierce when it comes to you and all that is good and true. Hey humanity cannot comprehend us but that's okay. We'll keep it real until they come to know the real and true truth of you.

Know that you are my dear and one day soon we will hold hands for the entire world to see.

Michelle and Michelle Jean

Good God we need the full truth. So why are you allowing the religious community to slander you like this?

Why do you allow them to use you in this manner?

Their god and gods are not you but yet humanity believe otherwise. Ethiopia gave you up to become a part of the etheran race and look at them today. Israel is not favoured by you. Your true people know this because the original Israelites were Ethiopians. No one can change this no matter the land and their deceit. **Hence Babylonians are identity thieves.** They will do anything to steal the identity of the Black Race without knowing the full truth and I am tired of this. I refuse them hence they are doing their all in the spiritual realm to steal my identity with you Good God and I will not have it. You need to put a stoppage to this right away. I told you, we need to be impenetrable in all that we do, so why the hell are you allowing these demon duppies to steal my financial wealth and health; life? Truth is not about hatred, so no one should steal my identity and wealth from me. So stop permitting this. Goodness in not evil, hence we and or our goodness should not be sacrificed to evil. We are not sacrificial lambs and no matter how I talk it seems stick pap inna you ease hole because you are not listening. **Stop sacrificing me to evil; I am fucking fed up of it. I am fucking fed up of**

them stealing my true and good rights (wealth and health; good prosperity) from me. Stop letting them hinder me from doing the good I truly need to do. Good God, my temper is fierce right now and if I let it go I will disrespect you brutally and I truly don't want or need this. I need to calm this brutal temper and you know this. So truly listen before I go more than ballistic on you. ***I did not choose death nor did I choose evil, so truly stop letting spiritual evil take my financial prosperity of goodness and truth; financial wealth and health from me come on now.*** Listen you know the lies these Babylonian Jews spread and tell and I refuse to be like them. I did not marry death, you married me to good and true life hence until death do we part. Meaning you will leave my ass if I do wrong and or wrong things. So truly don't with me because losing you is not an option. I am not them, so truly don't cast me in the same light and shadow as them. I more than unconditionally truly love you; so why would want them and or want their lies and deceit?

No wonder Revelations say, "BEWARE OF THE JEWS THAT CALL THEMSELVES JEWS BECAUSE THEY ARE OF THE ***SYNAGOGUE*** OF SATAN."

The full truth must be told because you do not base life on skin colour; tone. We are white and black because there is life and death and our skin colours just tell us what realm we are from. No forget that

MY MANY QUESTIONS TO GOD

because I am just going to confuse humanity on another level. Just know that there is a Black and White Death. Black Death is the one to take your spirit from the flesh and White Death is the final death; how your spirit dies.

Negative energy exist but we cannot just look at this. We have to look at universal life and the Universe is both black and white; a mixture of race and he cannot take sides. He must be fair and just in all that he does.

Listen Lovey, he (the universe) made sure I knew he was both black and white. So if anyone thinks of going to him with the I am white and I am entitled to you bullshit, is going to get laughed at and kicked out. This goes for blacks that will come with this bullshit. Hence skin colour can get us nowhere with the universe, earth and you Good God. So truly good luck to all of you that are saying Black is superior to White and White is superior to Black. You're all inferior hence there are not colour schemes when it comes to hue in the universe and the kingdom of Good God and Allelujah.

Wow I truly don't want to be any of you that pit race against race because none of you will get in.

So truly good luck to the religions of the world because the Universe, the Earth and Good God has a bone to pick with all of you. Thus saith the Lord thy God.

So truly good luck with your race cards because hell is waiting for the lots of you. Know that it (hell) will be your home until your jail and or prison sentence is over and your spirit dies; never to come back to life because there is **NO RESSURRECTION OF THE DEAD.** All of you racist bitches that think you won't be housed with blacks in hell had better truly think again. **NONE OF YOU HATH A SAY IN HELL, SO TRULY GOOD LUCK WITH YOUR RACIST FLAGS AND CARDS.** Laaade have mercy because mi affi laugh to regile. Damn I'd pay good money to see the lots of your racist asses in hell trying to weasel your way out of this one. Woe murda because the demons of hell is going to have a field day with the lots of you literally.

Life is real and we are to live life good and well; clean. We're not to fight for hell and or a place in hell but daily we do this. For what?

Come on tell me. Why the hell do you fight for a place in hell?

Death is not superior to life. Life is superior to death because true life cannot die only death can. Yes your evil and wicked life. The one you choose and chose here on earth.

<u>As humans we are to know that our skin tone represent the universe. Yes life and death also on a physical and spiritual level. But true life is not represented by colour because none of us know what true life is.</u>

Not one of us can represent true life in the physical realm due to sin; the wrongs that we do.

As humans we have to do better BECAUSE ENMITY WAS PUT BETWEEN MAN GLOBALLY BY WICKED AND EVIL PEOPLE AND THIS IS WRONG.

I refuse to hate you based on religion, skin colour (hue), sexual preference, hair colour, eye colour or whatever. I know wrong from right and it's the right that I must do daily not the wrong. Yes I loathe and hate certain things and I've told you this; but I will not dwell on hate or hate anyone because they don't like you or me. You are entitled to not like me but when you come with your violence and war bullshit, then I fucking draw the line. I will put you in your place. Keep your fucking god and gods of lies and deceit. Your god and gods is not superior to mine because mine do not pit anyone against anyone; nor does he tell you to go out and murder to rob another human being and or nation of their land and lands; what rightfully and truly belongs to them. I refuse all of you and your immigration bullshit. Fuck you and stay in your land with your death bullshit. See my borders, do not come near because the lots of you are all fucking condemned and without life. I need life and goodness for my land and people hence you are not fucking wanted nor are you needed and invited; so stay the fuck away from me. Come on now. **I respect my God and True Love so don't try to take him from me with your fucking lies. I MORE THAN INFINITELY TRULY DO NOT WANT WHAT YOUR GOD AND GODS HAVE. I AM MORE THAN HAPPY AND CONTENDED WITH MINE, SO TRULY FUCK OFF AND TRY YOUR SHIT WITH SOMEONE ELSE. DON'T COME BACK TO MY DOOR BECAUSE YOU WILL NOT LIKE THE CONSEQUENCES OF ME BECAUSE I WILL CUSS YOU RUDER THAN THIS.** My God knows this hence he knows he's secure in me and with me no matter how I cuss him and tell him he's not fair. **No, don't come try and take my good up, good up good food from me. Mi a Jamaican an certain things mi nuh play with and my true love is one of them.**

If you want to continue to choose death then so be it because it is your choice and right, but don't come around at the end a knocking at my door to let you in when the harvest comes. Trust me when you come I am hoping that you will not find my home. My home will be gone long before you can find it. When you come all you find is an empty space with no house and land.

This is why I tell Good God to close all gateways to him when his house and school is built. Yes I know where he wants me to be hence I will be in the Caribbean and Africa. Yes Russia too but why Russia I truly do not know.

It's time the saving game stop because as humans we do not choose Good God. We choose death, so death must save his and her people indefinitely.

As Blacks Good God can't keep coming to us and we keep rejecting him. He is going to pass you by and this has happened. We keep telling him we do not want saving and the offerings of death suits us fine, (the Jesus bullshit). Hence I tell you "HELL IS FULL OF BLACK PEOPLE AND RECRUITING MORE." This is how I saw it and this is how I am relating it back to you.

We all know religion was not designed to help man but to prophet whoops profit off man; humanity. Hence all religion tell you about their prophets; how they prophet

(profit) off capturing your soul and sending it to hell; so truly good luck to all of you.

This is humanities hell because you believed in lies and refuse to walk away from it.

You all know that hell is real but instead of walking away from hell, you accept the offerings of hell and expect someone to die to save you.

You erred, why should someone now sacrifice themself to save you? What makes you so important that I have to give up my life and the life of my family for you?

Evil wrote their law and laws to protect evil. Good does not have to because good is good and true all the time. I need to live in true peace and harmony, hence I choose good and true life over death and ask Good God and Allelujah, My True Love and Bestest of Friend to separate me and the good and true seeds including land and lands he's given me from all that is wicked and evil. This includes animals and spirits that are wicked and evil. I want and need none around me hence I have to secure an impenetrable life including foundations and frameworks with him Good God and Allelujah. Come on now.

Michelle and Michelle Jean

Wow because White Jesus this book is truly for you. Now I can speak about you and ask why?

Death surrounds you hence you are not of the physical realm, you are of the spiritual.

There is another in Russia claiming to be Jesus incarnate but Jesus did not exist over 2000 years ago. Jesus exists now and he is you.

You have the physical markings of death hence you are December born. You are of the dark side and horse, hence you do all for him. Your father is BLACK hence the Cajun in you. And I know many people will not comprehend this because when they look at you they see a white hue. But your bloodline goes deeper than hue hence humanity will not comprehend what I am talking about because they truly do not know nor do they truly know you.

Red, White and Blue is your flag. It's a very powerful flag hence your decent; the journey of your true family.

Wow White Jesus there is still a lot to learn about you because I wanted to talk about you but time including death would not permit me until now. **Yes the timing is right, hence White Russian Jesus step off because you are fake; not true. You are not White Jesus he is.**

You have not the true name of death nor are you from the spiritual realm. <u>*You cannot take this man's glory because whether humanity like it or not FRANCE HAS ALWAYS BEEN THE SEAT OF THE DEVIL.*</u> Power must go back to France. **How France use this power is now up to them. No, France has always been the seat of Good and Evil not just the seat of the devil.**

<u>**Yes the devil transferred power to Jay-Z but she can now take it from him and complete the ritual by handing power back to her land of decent which is France.**</u>

He can still take the throne of England yes, but that throne cannot stay in England it must go back to France because it was all about spiritual power not physical power.

Man I can't believe I missed it and although I cannot put it all together France and Greece can because Greece know the full truth and they have to speak it.

Do not even look at the churches because they did their own part and in truth I do not want to go into the book of the dead; Revelations to teach any of you. Put it together for yourself. And yes to you I am crazy and out of my head but it matters not what you think anymore because THE DEVIL WON OVER MAN – ALL OF HUMANITY. *Well not the children and people of Good God.*

The Jews can no longer hide the truth because power was never transferred and or belonged to Israel, it always belong to France but they kept quit.

Liberte is theirs hence the statue of Liberty; Her.

So White Jesus I congratulate you but truly good luck because my true and living God did not lose, your father did and remember the Jews – true Jews did defeat you.

Everything must now come into place hence France must live by the code of good and evil. And White Jesus stay the hell out of the South of France because this nick of the woods is not the devil's stomping ground or yard. I claim it hence you are duly warned.

Yes nothing makes sense hence I was missing something and I've found it.

There is a bigger picture that I cannot see hence I am going to leave it alone. So truly start using your true last name. And yes I am going to leave you alone because death is all around you. Hence this book belongs to death because death has been draining me whilst writing it.

Damn boy people truly don't know you. I talk about greater death but to actually see spiritual death in the living is beyond me because I did not think this was possible.

No wonder the universe wants to get rid of him. Damn boy people worship you because universal death is truly you.

You have the physical markings of death because you made sure you put them on your hands; body.

You are the circle of life because you crafted it, hence the life of death is on your back. You are universal because death lives everywhere on earth; hence the 4 corners of the globe and the 24000 years death had to rack up man's death; debts so that he can take them physically and spiritually to hell with him.

Yes this goes deeper but I will not interfere with you and your father because your death is that deadly.

Wow, you are cold and deep but yet humble as pie.

Underneath your facade lies the death angel of man's spirit; the spiritual realm. Yes I've just touched the hem of your garment because it is as white as snow.

You have spiritual power hence your death toll will be high and is high. Hence the billions that will die; must die shortly.

Your father did right by you but then humanity truly do not know you. We've been taught and trained to look the other way because we've been focusing on other lands America, Africa, Middle Eastern Lands. Hence your father did a good job to throw attention off the truth of you and France.

Yes I do not have all hence the Knights Templar's that must now protect and follow you.

Death surrounds you but this death is not physical but spiritual; universal because I saw you in the universe and I did see your teeth; hence teeth to me represent death; the death of you and or someone close to you.

You do all for your father hence your subliminal messages in your videos. You have the power hence anyone that is of a higher order knows you; the messages you give to your people; humanity.

Why 30STM?

Why Mars?

No don't answer that because Mars is the planet of death and is associated with Aries the God of War.

But is Mars truly the planet of death?

Yes you have to gather your people hence humanity is slated to die before 2032.

You are from a great family hence the Masonic Order. Well better put Metatron which is symbolic to your biological last name and not the one you use today. Hence he was one of the four and twenty elders of old. Yes the 24 elders of death. One thousand years each had to do the will of death hence the cycle of life is 1000 years for death and not true life. True life hath no ending but death has an end.

Yes there is more but on this day I will leave everything alone because my body is being drained.

Nothing is symbolic anymore and like I said, humanity must know the full truth. It matters not anymore because like I've said, THE DEVIL WON OVER HUMANITY – HUMANS. We did sin and we did FALL SHORT OF THE GLORY OF GOD – GOOD GOD.

<u>It matters not what the churches globally say anymore because they did their jobs and sealed the faith and or lives of billions in hell.</u> Billions cannot take their names out of the book of the dead; hence I will not interfere with your father's children. They are hell bound and rightfully so.

Like I've told Good God and Allelujah, I will not save wicked and evil people if I am the saving grace of the world because these people know what they have done. Evil will always seek to kill and they did kill. They sacrifice others to death hence paying death for the wrongs they have done. Come on White Jesus go back to one of the original students of death; Abraham being one of them. Did he not pay death a portion of his wealth?

And yes the offering and sacrifice was accepted. Abraham made a sacrifice unto Aries thus the ram not goat. So no matter how death mask the truth, the truth will be found. **<u>DEATH'S CHILDREN MUST SACRIFICE THEIR OWN UNTO DEATH. THEY MUST PERFORM DEATH RITUALS BY KILLING ANOTHER HUMAN BEING.</u>** This is the law and this law is still being carried out until this day. There is only one way into hell and one way out of hell and that is death. So truly good luck to the lots of you that has and have signed a pact with death.

But why the casket?

Yes it's the final resting place of the bones of man not flesh, but why a casket?

Do you need to rest now?

Ah White Jesus, you are handsome but you should have never cut your hair. I am so disappointed and yes I am fascinated by you. But I know the death of you; that which you bring.

So White Jesus really and truly?

Why now because you are no Joker?

There is nothing funny about death but then again people will not comprehend you and me. Life and death. They are baffled and saying what the fuck? Yes you white people because many of you still cannot comprehend life; this universe on a physical and spiritual level.

So Jared this book truly belongs to you because death truly surrounds you. And yes Love is blind but true love can never be blind because it's the truth. Hence I need not say more.

Michelle

MY MANY QUESTIONS TO GOD

My body is being drained Good God and I truly cannot take the draining anymore. You know the truth of life and this madness on earth have to stop.

You have to stop it because lives are being lost daily and this is truly not right.

There should be no beef and or strife between North and South nor should there be beef and or strife between South and North. This fighting is bullshit and you know it. Lives are being lost like I've said and it must stop because this has nothing to do with man. It has to do with North and South and the struggle for power by the North. **<u>The North wants full control of everything and this cannot be. Life is not about death it's about life and humans should not be involved in BROTHER TO BROTHER AND OR SISTER TO SISTER AND OR SISTER TO BROTHER WARFARE.</u>** If two family members cannot get along; then separate and go your own way in peace not pieces come on now.

Why should humans be caught up in all of this. You of yourself said you love us so, but yet watch us make the wrong choices each and every day. You watch us die without stopping the bullshit.

I keep talking about Black Babies being fed to alligators as gator bait in the United States. You saw this happen

and did nothing. I don't give a bleep about choice because no one should live with evil.

No one should have to choose between good and evil.

No one should have to live to die.

None of us should have been born with the genes of sin in the first place. You are capable of correcting the wrong that was done to man – humanity and you refuse to.

Don't tell me about messengers right now because I am so frigging angry at you right now. I know the influence of signs in the spiritual realm hence I am dreaming about them now. I am seeing these signs and this man has them on his back.

He has them on his arm like me but mine was engrained not tattooed on. Good life is given Lovey, so why are we not living life good and true? Yes it's easy to fall from grace but was all of this called for?

What point does death have to make?

HAS HE (DEATH) NOT PROVEN TO YOU TIME AND TIME AGAIN THAT HUMANS ARE NOT LOYAL TO YOU?

So why are you standing in the way of death when it comes to his pay?

The sins of man rightfully belong to death; so give it to him because it's his and her right when it comes to humans. You cannot interfere any longer because like I said, if I am the saving grace for humanity, I will never ever save anyone that is wicked and evil. Wicked and evil people know the evils that they have done. I know the pain of lies and deceit Good God. I lived it literally only to find out at the end that I was the intended target of death. And I say to you now with goodness and truth; true peace, to let it be done now. I cannot watch and or see anymore death. I am tired of it, truly tired. My body cannot go through anymore and you know it. I am weak and I need strength. **Truly let death and their people go because DEATH HAS THEIR OWN PLANET.**

Death must take their people home and you are blocking the way. **Billions did not choose you, so truly let them live with the choice they've made. You cannot continue to keep these people here on earth because they truly do not belong to you.**

YOU CANNOT KEEP SENDING MESSENGERS AND HUMANS KEEP REJECTING THEM. LEAVE THEM ALONE. DO NOT SEND ANYMORE MESSENGERS TO SAVE THEM.

DEM NUH WANT YU SO LEF DEM.

Death is the choice of humans so leave them to death. They trust death over you; so let it go because you were not their good and true choice; death is.

Yu get plug out and log out.

Humans have tuned you out. You are no longer a part of their electrical grid. Dem move on to another grid that suits them just fine. Hence their solar panels are not turned to you, it's turned to the sun; fire.

You are not their wind turbines and or technology; suh lef dem mek dem tan.

I am tired of quarreling with you for your own damned good hence AMBITION GOES A FAR AND LONG WAY. Lef ambitionless people alone. You know if a person wants better they will do better for self; hence the good we do for self and others. You've done all the good you can for humanity and humanity dash eee way, suh lef dem.

Ole people sey, wanti wanti caane get eee and getti getti nuh want it and this is so true. Look how long mi a cry to yu and yu a ignore mi. What is so precious about death's children that you have to be ignoring your own?

What is so precious about death's children that you have to be making sacrifices to death with the lives of your own people?

Yes death is strong but death is not stronger than life – true life because at the end of the day, death dies but life – true life lives on; is eternal.

Yes you need to be reminded of this. If a man does not want saving you cannot save them. You know this and I am reminding you of this and telling you this. If we have no ambition for self, how the hell can we expect you to have ambition for us?

If we constantly choose death over life, how can you save us?

Have not the Black Race done this to you time and time again?

You send messengers to save them time and time again because they are the first race messengers go to to save and time and time again and they keep choosing death over you.

Did I not go to America and ask for help and was rejected?

Did not my own reject me?

So life keep rejecting life hence there is nothing we can do because the black race keep telling you time and time again they truly do not want saving. So move on because they keep rejecting you hence you are rejected. Truly do not answer their calls anymore. Change your phone number and cell number come on now. Di only time dem call a when dem want something and as soon as dem get it dem gone. Who are you to them?

Think and live. Yes I bug you. But who would you rather me bug? I bug you for everything including bug you with my devotional, songs and overflow of true love. Hence you know how special you are to me in all that I do. So truly let death be done with me on the spiritual and physical level. Please let them stop taking our good and true prosperity from us in the physical and spiritual realm. Come on now.

I've told you in another book that Death and or Satan can put im pat pan eee fiya and rest assured the black race is going to sell you out and reject you. Why do you think HELL IS FULL OF BLACK PEOPLE AND RECRUITING MORE?

Death knew that the Black Race would not accept you. They would cling to him because he offers them more. Hence the Voodoo and Obeah; all the evil bullshit that they do is so prevalent in Black Culture and Societies.

Eve (Evening) fell for the bullshit and failed; died because of what? We fail to see the light in the darkness and the darkness in the light. We cannot comprehend the lights; different lights hence we fail.

Good does not need chemistry to alter because no one can alter the good of man; our true genes which is our spirit.

Evil can be altered hence man use chemicals; the chemicals of science and land (physical and spiritual) to alter man; their genes and or DNA; flesh.

Thus evil will always seek to destroy; change all that do not belong to them.

Evil will always capture because evil dwell on capture land and lands.

Evil will always lie and kill because this is how evil keep going.

Evil will always defame because evil seek fame; lasting impressions.

Evil will always be evil because there is absolutely no good in evil and will never be.

Evil hath not good life hence evil dies after a time. Thus we were told, "THE WAGES (PAY) OF SIN IS DEATH." SO BECAUSE WE SIN, WE HAVE TO PAY DEATH AND OR SIN WITH OUR LIVES.

And no matter how you show this to man – humanity, man – humanity still cannot learn.

Yes death has his and her children hence the sins and or evils of man outweigh any good that they can or will do. Yes this is sad; hence the price man pays for their wickedness on a daily basis. No, they cannot see this but each sin and each good is record for all to see. Hence woe be unto humanity shortly literally.

No, I will not fight with death or for death because I know the lies of man; the lies humanity tell to feed death and their ego.

You also know my heartache and pain hence I am asking you to truly let it be over.

Do not prolong the life of death anymore because the pain and suffering is not worth it. Yes many gave their lives over to death willingly, but what about those that did not?

The innocent should not have to pay with their lives despite the sins of the fathers and mothers. No child should have to live to pay for their parent's debt come on now. This is not just nor is it fair to them because like I've told you in another book, we do commit sin (s) of our own.

Generational sins no one should have to pay for but yet these sins are handed down from generation to generation.

If a child or anyone say, Good God and Allelujah I choose you then let them live. Help them to truly live for you by taking evil from their hearts and DNA here in the living – physical realm. The spiritual realm keep them clean because you and I both know that the life you live in the physical determines where you go in the spiritual.

Evil should not come in contact with us once we've chosen you.

Evil should not take away our prosperity once we've chosen you come on now. Evil should not have a right to do this but yet you let this constantly happen to me.

Evil should always step back and be on their merry little way. Evil was not chosen, so evil cannot come into our home (s) and domain. Come on now.

You are Lovey but yet you fail to recognize this.

Evil is self centered and cocky hence Aries love to fight, refuse to accept when he's wrong come on now.

I can't keep talking to you for the better good of you and our people. Come on now.

You have to let go and finish the process. You cannot stand in death's way any longer. If you do, you cannot complain when death takes it all. You are hindering them.

Nobady nuh want yu suh lef dem to wey dem want.

Damn why can't you learn this. Stop begging for a frigging place with humans that truly don't want you.

Yu a begga? Yes I beg you because I prefer all my goodness to come from you. You are truly valued by me and mi nuh like begga people even though I beg you. And yes I've lashed out at you for this because I truly don't like to beg you. To me you should provide all of my asking that I ask of you. And don't you dare go there because yu dumpling sweet. Let's not figet di Millie and breadfruit too.

Dem lef yu alone so have some frigging ambition fi self and move on. Stop letting death and their people laugh afta yu seaka ungrateful and deceitful people – humans.

You are not their ring of choice. Meaning billions did not commit to you in truth. Dem jus a use yu fi kip dem life.

Look at the bloodshed on land. Now tell me was all of it worth it?

Look into yourself and tell me if this; the bloodletting and sacrifice what you ordained for man – humanity?

Now tell me why I should not lash out at you and call you unjust and unfair?

Billions are going to die because of you and them. So tell me what part of loving us so is you; death?

The choice of humanity is truly not you, so stop sacrificing you and your people including your reputation for people that did not choose you. They are not your people so truly let them go. Do not extend the lifeline anymore because I am tired, Mama Africa is tired and the universe wants to get rid of him. So truly look into yourself and see; yes tell me if prolonging the life of death and their people worth it?

Look at the cost and tell me if it's truly worth it.

Tell me if it's truly worth saving people that truly don't want to be saved, people who have chosen death over you?

DEATH IS VALUED YOU ARE NOT.

DEATH HAS THE FINAL SAY IN THE LIVES OF MAN – HUMANITY AND NOT YOU. (Our sin and sins)

So why are you holding out on hope, false hope? Save your own in goodness and truth because these are the people that truly love you and care about you.

Why feed death when death wants to take care of his and her own?

What sense does that make? Death wants their people and you are hindering them. Then if I was death, I would bring you before your own council and charge you Good God and Allelujah for THEFT.

Yes I went there. You do not stop death from taking their rightful people. Hence I have learned that death does not relinquish what is theirs so easily. And yes I know death can be stopped but what right do we have to continue to do this. Yes I've done this hence death did try to take me. So yes I am stepping aside and let death deal with their own people.

This is what they want and we must give it to them because this is the right of death.

PEOPLE DID PAY TO DIE HENCE OUR SINS. Thus the wages (pay) of sin is death.

Lovey we cannot interfere anymore and you know this.

People choose death; it's their choice so truly leave them alone.

I truly do not want to miss the mark with you hence I told you the full truth must be known. You now have to learn to accept the decision and decisions of man – humanity.

If humanity respected you, they would not choose death over you all the time.

If humanity wanted life – good and true life for themself they would not accept death, they would accept and choose good life so that they can live.

So truly step aside and let what needs to be done be done come on now.

Michelle and Michelle Jean

It's March 13, 2015 and Good God I forgive you.

I truly forgive you because I am so not like you and never will be.

I've come to realize there's no fairness in your world because you allow and permit evil to hurt your children.

You permit and allow your children to go through hell and I've faced hell in my life. Hence I ask you why?

Have to ask what I've done you for you to constantly permit wicked and evil people to hurt me without cause.

What have I done to you for you to want the devil and their children to do all to break me?

Good God why?

Is this your form of truth and true love when it comes to me?

Is this your true hatred of me?

Why me?

What have I done to you for you to hurt me in this way?

It's March 13, 2015 and I dreamt an old friend of mine. Someone I went to school with and was close to because I use to run away from my home and go to live with them. (Rommel)

Good God why?

Why now after all these years?

Yes I want to cry but cannot because I knew I was to fall and have nothing in life.

I've talked to you about this and complained to you about this.

I told you I am prepared to fall now because I cannot go anymore. <u>But to dream this, this morning – dream Rommel telling me this lady that we knew tied me so that I could not rise is beyond me.</u>

He tied me.
She tied me.

<u>**Now I ask you, what did I do to her that was evil for her to tie me so that I would have nothing in life?**</u>

I would struggle financially and end up begging in the streets. Wicked people Good God, wicked people, wicked people and you allow this. Wow because you are truly unbelievable. *You permit evil and we are to turn to you for a saving grace in the end after you prostitute us out to death and evil. Come on now.*

We are to truly love you after you've sacrificed us to evil?

We are to live clean when you give us all that is dirty. And don't you dare say how dare you because I have a right to ask this of you. You take our sanity from us and expect us to be okay when we are truly not okay. So how....no I won't swear at you. How do you expect us to feel?

Tell me because what you do to us is truly wrong; hurtful. It cause us pain, hence you should not sacrifice us to death; we are not death's children. Let death and his children be because you and your people have nothing to prove. Death writes laws to please and suit them and I will not do this, write laws to suit your children and people because there's none to be written. All I ask of you is for you to take evil from us infinitely and indefinitely forever ever so that we can live good and clean with you. I have no need for wicked and evil people hence I include them not in our world of goodness and truth.

This has nothing to do with hue but has all to do with cleanliness and truth; goodness. No one should have to lie to come to you.

No one should have to live unclean to get to you.

No one should have to die to come to you. All of this is death's doing not life's doing; you. You have to be just and fair and take death out of the equation of good and true life. True and pure love is attainable; it's man – humanity that do not want the truth. They want all the offerings of death hence they kill to maintain it. (Sacrifices)

I will not live like this and you know this, so why the hell are you not shutting down spiritual wickedness?

Why are you letting them take all from me?

You are truly unbelievable because you cannot comprehend impenetrable frameworks and foundations when it comes to me and my truth and goodness of you and our people and worlds; lands.

<u>No, I cannot turn from you because I know hell and what wicked people can do in the living. You don't have to hurt anyone for people to hurt you.</u>

Rommel told me her name but I told him I could not remember her. He said you know her but like I said, I could not remember her. He told me she died and she wanted to see me. Seeing me was her confession, she wanted to confess to me what she had done but she could not find me; reach me.

Good God, I've done her nothing so tell me how could you permit this; permit my hurt and pain like this?

Now tell me, how can I forgive someone like this? Hence I echo my pain throughout the earth and universe as well as your realm; kingdom and abode by saying; I will never ever forgive her for this.

<u>No forgiveness is in my heart for her nor is there any in my heart for Obeah and Voodoo workers; workers of iniquity. I remember my hurt, my pain and how I lashed out at you in anger. So no.</u>

<u>I forgive you but I will never forgive her or any iniquity worker because what she did was not called for. You do not hurt people that have done you nothing in life.</u>

I do not seek to hurt people. All I've ever wanted was to help others but she took that away from me in many ways. But in truth she didn't fully take my glory because I still help others and it matters not if that help is encouraging someone on a daily basis.

Hence I've told you time and time again Good God that I will never help anyone that is wicked and evil.

I more than infinitely and indefinitely lock them out of our good and true world.

The mountains of LA and Nevada still stand Good God. I will never forgive you for this because the mountain is ours, and no human, spirit or animal has the right to destroy them. I truly love you more than unconditionally, but will never forgive you for this nor will I ever forgive her for tying me.

<u>**Her confession means nothing to me hence death has her ass in hell and I truly care not how death and the demons of hell inflict punishment on her. I step aside because like I said, no forgiveness ever is granted by me for her and him also. You don't hurt people that have done nothing to you. Let hell be her forever ever home because she did wrong and no forgiveness is in my heart for her and him.**</u>

No forgiveness is in my heart for wicked and evil people and inequity workers, including wicked and evil spirits that carry out the wicked and evil deeds of those in the living.

You hurt me and My God Lovey, my true best friend and you seek forgiveness from me by your confession before you died. Seek none from me because none is truly given.

You caused me true pain.
You caused me to cuss my baby.
You caused me true anger and pain. You rocked me; took all from me willingly and willfully and now you seek forgiveness from me by confessing what you have done to me. Bitch guh suckout wey nuh lef inna Satan and di demons of hell an lef mi alone. You fucking hurt me and my family, including my God. Truss mi death has all authority to make your life in hell more than a living and spiritual hell. Seek no forgiveness from me because I give none. This is my true and good will when it comes to me and My Lovey including family and people, the true and good seeds he has and have given me for what you have done to me. I condemn you and All Iniquity Workers, Obeah man and woman, voodoo priest and priestesses including all that tie people, and set duppy pan people, tun dung people to hell infinitely and indefinitely. This condemnation is global as well as indefinite and solid; can never be broken more than indefinitely. Yes my anger is there, but I have a right to do this. You do not hurt people like this come on now. I've done you nothing and you hurt me and my family like this. You took all from me financially and you expect me to forgive you. Oman nuh mek mi cuss out wey no lef a yu tiday you hear. I have

absolutely no respect for you because you are an iniquity worker that takes money to hurt others and for this you are condemned all around.

My family and me almost ended up in the streets in the dead of winter. Now tell me how fair was that to me and them? My kids bitch, my children and you expect me to forgive you. Mi suffa with dem. You knew my sufferation and now you have the gaul to ask forgiveness of me? I would rather forgive Lovey for the decay and ruined mountains of LA and Nevada rather than forgive you.

KNOW THIS; I WILL NEVER EVER TURN THE OTHER CHEEK FOR ANYONE INCLUDING SPIRITS THAT IS/ARE WICKED AND EVIL COME ON NOW.

I've had to borrow, bug my family at times for help just to put food on the table for my children to eat.

You left me with nothing.

You broke me because not even shoes and panty I could buy.

Not even food I could buy.

MY MANY QUESTIONS TO GOD

My kids went to school with holes in the bottom of their shoes in winter because I could not buy shoes for them.

I was more than abused by him hence the abuse I took is known in the spiritual realm. It is talked about also. I had to walk around with an eye patch and yes we talked about this.

My rent I could not afford.

Not even a winter jacket I could afford to go to work when I was able. Hence I still have my son's winter hoodie that I wear until this day including pants.

You left me with nothing but I had something, I had my true love that I blast. Hence I truly and unconditionally stand by him and my wonderful and beautiful mother and hold their hands and say truly thank you for saving me and being there in the storm and storms with me. I truly more than love you infinitely and indefinitely forever ever without end and I save you, truly save you both because you're both with me in all I've done and been through.

I will never be ungrateful to any of you. I remember goodness hence I truly have to save you both.

This woman did her job yes but Lovey you and my mother is my stay. When he came to kill me with his smoke; fire, my mother was there to hold my hand.

He was warned but he refuse to listen hence hell is consuming him right now. Thus with every fabric of my being I will never ever save him.

Let him burn because I extend no goodness or lifeline to him, nor do I extend one to anyone who is wicked and evil including her; this demon woman that tied me.

Stay in hell because "THE WAGES OF SIN IS DEATH," hence all who are wicked and evil must face hell infinitely and indefinitely. No forgiveness will I ever give to wicked and evil people including spirits that knowingly and willingly hurt others for money, personal gain, sacrifice, sport, plain out wickedness and evil. They are wicked and evil and they know what they have done; are doing.

People has and have killed themselves because of you.

People suffered because of you.

Children; families were left mother and fatherless because of you.

Lovey look at the hurt and pain that I feel for losing my mother.

Look at my fears of losing you.

Yes the tears come but I have to hold them back.

Yes I cling to you but my pain was and still is more than I can bare.

Hence no, I cannot forgive her nor can I or will I make any provisions for wicked and evil people including spirits because I truly want them gone infinitely and indefinitely without end from everywhere.

It's over now because now I can rise and better serve well have fun with you.

Truly thank you and my mother for being there for me and with me.

True love always because both of you are dear to me.

So let's do it. Let's acquire our, well your 25 million dollar mega mansion because it's time for me to heal and truly move on with you.

So as I take your hand and my mother's hand including the hands of the true and good seeds you've given me and those who I hold dear, the land of Jamaica not the people, Kenya, China, Africa – the Southern Lands of Africa except for South Africa, The Cayman Island, British Columbia and all the good people that helped me. I take your hands now in true goodness and truth, prosperity, cleanliness, honesty, true peace and tranquility, true love and walk with you all to Good God and Allelujah in glory. Goodness, true goodness is in me for all of you and I now save you in goodness and in truth. I have to because of goodness and true will. We will walk together to Zion infinitely and indefinitely forever ever in goodness and in truth without end.

I have to remember goodness Good God and Lovey and yes I still do not know why Russia but I am going to leave this alone. And yes let there be an exercise clause that if any of these lands fail you and or continue with evil then they must be evicted from our goodness right away infinitely and indefinitely. I refuse all facet of evil and it's time we now live good and true; clean and put away all that is wicked and evil indefinitely forever ever infinitely without end. I do not need the hatred anymore so all that is hateful and spiteful; wicked must go indefinitely without end.

The pain and hurt is great Good God so now wicked and evil people must weep and moan; know their end because of the wickedness they have done.

No Lovey I will not lay my life down or on the line for anyone because you gave me something that is precious and that is the gift of true and good life; truth and I have to cherish it. I have to live and do all the good that I can for us and our people. So truly thank you for not letting me go in my time and times of need.

You did help me hence I have to stay with you no matter how I tell you we are through in my anger and frustration.

You are truly good Lovey hence you are my Darling and True Friend.

When all others fail you've never failed me. You kept me Lovey because death did all to kill me.

So truly thank you because I save you, truly save you and my mother and all those who I hold true and dear to me.

So on this day March 13, 2015 seal my good and true intentions with you Good God and let my good will towards you, my mother, the land and lands you've given me and our good and true people be carried out infinitely and indefinitely without end. Good health, wealth, prosperity, true peace, honesty, cleanliness and good will for all Good God without end. An abundance of food, clean water, wealth and health be for all forever ever without end.

Good God truly remember my good and true intentions and will for Jamaica and not the wicked and evil people.

Kenya the land and people but not the wicked and evil people.

China the land and people but not the wicked and evil people.

Russia the land and people but not the wicked and evil people.

The Cayman Islands because this is where you want and need our vacation home to be. Truly remember the land and good people and do all that you need to do to cleanse this land of all that is wicked and evil.

The Southern lands of Africa truly remember these lands but the wicked and evil people remember them not. Also, as I have no true good will for South Africa so truly remember them not. Remember Nelson Mandela and how they South Africans imprisoned him in hell – the jailhouse of hell for trying to save his good and true people. So truly save Nelson Mandela because he did try. Save his people but all others save them not because I save none.

Ah Lovey, remember Scotland and France – Southern France (Lyon) because these lands are truly dear to me.

Lovey, never forget British Columbia because this land and or province is of my true good will but not Toronto for some strange reason.

My Darling, if I am incorrect in my asking please truly forgive me and let me correct my wrongs.

No Babylonian land will I save. So for the rest of the lands in the globe truly good luck because I am truly not with you. Yes I can name them for you but many of you know who you are by now.

Michelle and Michelle Jean
March 13, 2015

MY MANY QUESTIONS TO GOD

It's March 14, 2015 and the power is out again. Many people are without power and it's winter.

What's going on Good God? This is the second time in less than a month that we are having a major outage.

I'm also dreaming about California virtually each and every day.

Good God, I keep dreaming about the Kardashians and I truly do not know why.

Lovey, California reminds me of Jamaica and yes both lands are unclean because when Death talk about sin they talk about the United States of America.

Lovey I have to get to the Cayman Islands and soon. You know my financial situation so please truly help me.

She tied me and she is dead, so why am I not released from the clutches of hell financially; her tie Good God?

Why did you permit her to tie me in the first place?

Did you know see and know the pain that this would cause?

Lovey, you cannot continue to allow wicked and evil people to hurt your children and people; family.

We are your family Good God so treat us as such and do better for us and only us.

You cannot continue to prostitute us out to death any longer. This is not fair nor is it just come on now. You are willing to sacrifice us for what?

What does death have that you want? And don't you dare say an abundance of people. Remember **will,** hence it's a person's right; good and true right not to choose you.

Value you, your name and people and truly protect us. No one should have to hurt us or keep us down come on now.

No one should have to hinder us and our good progress. This isn't fair to us nor is it fair to life come on now.

Michelle and Michelle Jean

You know its funny how I talk about forgiveness but yet I truly cannot forgive her for what she did. I cannot find it in my heart to forgive her. Maybe I am wrong in some way but how do you truly forgive someone that willingly hurt you for no reason?

How do you grasp this and turn the other cheek and say, I am the bigger and better person because in all you did, you could not kill me; take my life?

What did I do to her for her to tie me and now that she knows her hell she wants me to forgive her? It matters not if she's dead, the tie is still there; it's not broken. When evil tie you to death, that tie is unbreakable in some ways. Yes I want to get mad at Good God for permitting this but somehow I can't, and I truly do not know why. Yes I know he's with me and kept me safe but how can another human being do this to someone?

How can anyone forgive evil?

I can't because I think of the others she has done this to.

I am thinking of the children that cry for their parent.

Those that would give anything for their father and mother to say happy birthday, I love you.

MY MANY QUESTIONS TO GOD

When someone ties you they tie you for life. They tie you so that you go mad and die and some have and has died. So because of this, I truly cannot forgive her in anyway.

To me Good God and family, evil is not deserving of forgiveness because they do all to kill you, take life from you; all. So yes I can say I am a hypocrite for this. But what child should go hungry because of another human beings ills; wickedness?

Yes I tell Lovey and Good God to let wicked and evil people go because they did not choose him. He should not sacrifice himself and his people for these demons because the pain is great.

I lash out at him and yes I am brutally upset that he allowed someone to tie me so that I would end up in the streets with nothing. People and family, you truly don't know about spiritual wickedness. When I talk and or write you think me foolish but who feels it knows it. No one should have to face this type of hell come on now. This goes beyond wickedness and hatred. Trust me it's not me alone that has been tied by evil. Truly speak to a Jamaica or anyone from the Caribbean, Africa and India and they will tell you of the wickedness of man; the evils that some people do to keep you down; trampled down. Some send blow fi yu. Suh if a man sey dem wi guh a Jamaica fi yu know that they are going to Obeah yu. They are going to go to Jamaica to obeah yu. If a man tell yu sey dem a throw blow fi yu, know that dem a goh a obeah man or oman fi yu. When a man or woman tell you dem a throw blow fi yu, it means they are going to kill you. And doctor caane fine how dem kill you because doctors can't track the blows of the dead. There's no technology that I know of for this. So truly don't let these churches fool you because some of them dabble in witchcraft or Obeah. Hence nuff parchment paper sell. Some a unnu waane lef unnu wife or husband and can't because unnu tie. Hence truly be careful who you eat from and who you lend your clothes to. Certain powda anno baby powda darling, hence the evils that some participate in. A lot of you don't know that the dead walk amongst the living; hence the churches globally tell you bullshit about the dead. Some people can see the dead as plain as day. Meaning as they see you perfectly they see ghost perfectly.

Some, the dead do talk to them; tell them things. Hence there are dark angels amongst us. I will not elaborate on this because you will not know what I am talking about. Certain things you are not to know hence my body is being drained writing this book. So because of this I will leave certain things alone.

Hence voodoo for some is a religion; practiced in Africa and some parts of the Caribbean openly.

So no for what she did to me I truly cannot forgive nor will I forgive her.

I've done her nothing and she took all from me. She did all to break and kill me. Hence I know the truth and God I look to for a saving grace. So because of this and more I truly cannot forgive her.

I cannot in good faith forgive her, I must condemn her and I've done this. She's in hell and looking to me to forgive her for what she's done to me. No, I cannot because I am sure I am not the only one she has done this to.

She has to face her own hell for what she did. So no, I will not save her from hell and this is my true and good will. Lovey did not have to go through my brutality come on now. She tried to take him from me family. Do you how much I over love him?

Do you know how precious he is to me? So no, every iniquity worker must be punished and condemned and I've done this. None must have a place with Good God and Allelujah come on now. None must have a saving grace because they hurt people for profit; monetary gain, and this I will never ever forgive. I forgive them not; hence hell must prepare a home for all workers of iniquity because I am fed up of them. I truly do not care what lodge of evil they are from Good God; none must have a place with you. They must go to hell and stay in hell come on now.

No one should have to feel pain for choosing you and you know this but yet you allow garbage like this to happen to us. I am tired of the bullshit I have to go through with you at the hands of wicked and evil people and spirits. Let it be over because I did ask you for impenetrable frameworks and foundations for us and our good and true people. It means evil must never ever forever ever never ever more than infinitely and indefinitely penetrate us or come near to us. We can no longer falter Lovey come on now.

You are my keep but you constantly let spiritual wickedness steal from you. Stop letting them steal my prosperity and you from me. I am fed up of this. You are my keep so bleeping keep me come on now. How would you feel if you lost me?

How?

Yes I am getting upset. This is me we are talking about. Stop hindering me because I have nothing to prove to death. If death is your brother he can kiss my natural brown ass. And I know he's smiling because I am the only one that can tell him this. Death stop interfering with me because you know I can make you lose it all.

Remember the wages of sin is death and I will dangle this before you. Stop letting your people hinder me because I no longer hinder you. Your people is your people and I do not want or need any in the kingdoms and abode of me and Good God. Leave me the fuck alone because I am tired of your bullshit. You have all you need so fucking take your people and go. Leave me and the good and true seeds that Good God has and have given me the fuck alone. Go already because you have all right and rights to take your people. Humanity did hand over self to you, so truly go. Good God and I can no longer interfere because billions did choose you over him.

Please just go in peace; true peace and take your people with you never to ever return again. You are not wanted on earth so please go to your home planet and stay there. You are evicted from the lands of earth because you did not create this universe hence the universe wants you gone as well. So truly go.

Michelle

You know something Good God in all of my abuse of you. And don't you dare say ya think. I have to ask, do you forgive evil?

Can you forgive evil for what they have done to humanity on earth and in the spiritual realm?

Can you forgive evil for what evil has done to you and your people?

You knew I was the intended target of death but yet you did not stop death, why?

I talk about trust and trusting you but yet you could not prevent death and his people from hurting me.

Yes I know I am still living and I thank you for that and a lot more but why?

Why did I have to go through this?

Why did my children have to go through this?

Why does anyone that is seeking you truthfully have to go through pain and suffering; hurt?

I know many are called and you gave them power to heal and help others and they've abused it. Yes you have trust issues, but you did not have to let them break me in this way man come on now.

You didn't have to make me feel so much pain.
Yes I know what about your pain?

What about the lies humanity has told on you?

Yes I see the crap on earth of man saying they love you but hate you; cannot truly love you. I know your pain and sufferings of people saying they praise and worship you but instead of living clean, they lie with the devil and do all for the devil each and every day. So yes I know the magnitude of your hurt and pain.

We say we love you and love life but yet pay to die.

We say we love but yet have not charity when it comes to others in society.

But Good God, am I any different from the rest of society? I truly don't want to help everyone in society. Why should I help the devil's children to continue to slaughter, slander and kill you and our people?

They mock you already, so why would I join them and continue with the lying and deceiving trend?

What would that prove? I cannot be like the rest of your messengers hence I am one away. I stick to you and self because in all that I do, I cannot fail me nor can I fail you even if I think I've failed. When it comes to my true and unconditional, more than unconditional love of truth of you, I cannot fail because this truth, true love is real hence you reside in me.

I've devoted myself to you and I have to live with my decision and truth because truth is everlasting life and I need everlasting life, I do not need death.

Yes my road is rough and yours is rough also. All I can do is imagine Lovey because what we do to you is truly not fair nor is it just.

Hence humans love for a reason in different seasons. Love fades but true love will never fade, cannot fade because it's true; real.

Like I said, I cannot be like everyone else hence you need to reinstate my prosperity and stop letting the spiritual wicked steal my wealth and you from me. You gave me something good, no one in the spiritual realm or the physical realm should hinder me from living good and true with you. Nor should they hinder me and your people from getting and achieving the good prosperity you've given us.

None of us came into this world to suffer but yet we suffer.

I didn't come into this world to suffer or die at the hands of wicked and evil people including spirits, so truly shut spiritual wickedness down infinitely and indefinitely forever ever without end.

The spiritual wicked can no longer aid the physical wicked Good God. Do something because your people are not the children of death, so death should not hinder us or stop us from praising and prospering with you. Like I said, you permit bullshit to happen to us and this is wrong.

Yes death wrote their law and laws to protect their own but what about the protection of your people Good God? Why continue to let us live like the defeated?

Why let us feel defeated?
What we don't matter to you?

You are truth Lovey and no evil should override your truth come on now.

Michelle

Lovey humans are different.
I am different.
Have to be different.

I know you do not lock anyone out of your good and true about but Good God was all this wickedness and evil worth it?

Lovey, you are my keep so why do you allow people; wicked and evil spirits to constantly hurt me?

Why is my life forbidden? Meaning susceptible to pain by wicked and evil people including spirits.

Yes I forgive you but you can't punish me for not forgiving you for the mountains of LA and Nevada. Yes you are angry at me but you cannot under any circumstances continue to allow humans to destroy earth. Yes I know there's a massive tsunami and or water destruction coming. This cannot be helped because we as humans were the wicked ones.

Yes family will get caught up in this mess, but it's the price they are going to pay for not truly listening. I need to be on my way to the Cayman Islands, so please whatever you do, help me to get the money so I can go.

Michelle

MY MANY QUESTIONS TO GOD

Good God I refuse to pray for the people of Jamaica. Dem too wicked and evil, so let them suffer in their condemnation.

They had many beatings in the forms of earthquakes (tsunami – Port Royal) and hurricanes and dem nah listen. So truly let destruction come, I pity them not.

I pray for them not anymore, hence I will extend no lifeline to di wicked and evil dem.

Nuff obeah man and oman dey pan ee island. Mek dem tun back death if dem can.

Obeah death mek death nuh come.

No Lovey nuh laugh. The wickedness of the people dem muss stop. You can't rape young kids and kill them daily and not think sey retribution naugh guh come.

You cannot have a corrupt government and government officials that sell out di lan an people dem to Death/Satan and not think retribution will not come.

You cannot live by the eat a food mentality by accepting dirty money to kill your own and not think that retribution won't come.

You can't sell your children to the highest bidder (human and child trafficking) and not think that retribution won't come.

You cannot bleach your skin and accept death – spiritual death in the living and not think retribution won't come.

You cannot rape your own children (incest) and not think that retribution won't come.

You cannot praise Satan and tattoo your skin like the demons of hell and not think retribution won't come.

You cannot build churches – homes unto death and think retribution won't come.

Jamaica had your flag and name; your good and true life Good God and they tainted you. Hence your name and flag; life have and has been taken from them and given back to you.

Look how many keep the order of death and profess Selassie as their god. So mek Selassie and di demons of hell save them because they the people sold you out.

Look at how many artists and politicians that sold their souls – spirit to be a part of lodge man society.

Nuff, sarry all a dem sell dem soul and sacrifice their own to death.

Family kill family
Fren kill fren
Pawsta kill congregation
Politicians sell out and kill the people and resources of the land they preside over.

So tell me, how can I continue to pray and plead with you for wicked and evil people Good God?

Let the sufferation begin. Did you not evict Eve (Evening) out of your kingdom?

Did you not deem Jamaica unclean? So why now would I stand in the way of death from destroying and taking dem wicked and evil people? I KNOW THEM NOT! HENCE I TURN MY BACK ON THEM AND ALL WHO ARE WICKED AND EVIL GLOBALLY. NONE CAN OR WILL STAND IN THE CONGREGATION OF THE RIGHTEOUS BECAUSE I AM SICK AND TRIED OF THEM AND THEIR EVILS; THE EVILS THAT THEY DO DAILY.

Jamaica had you Lovey and lost you. They gave you up to continue on their wicked pathway. Israel gave you up and Judah gave you up. So why the hell should I continue to have mercy for any of them come on now? We had yu and dash yu wey fi wah?

The cries of death has and have been echoed Good God, hence truly save your true own and leave the devil's children and people alone. Let Death go with them. Spare none because they are not your own. The law specifically say, **"THE WAGES OF SIN IS DEATH."** So uphold the law and stop breaking it. Humanity gave themselves over to death willingly and you can no longer interfere.

<u>You continue to do this, then death will have all authority to take your people and you know this because death has done this. Death has taken your people because you continue to let us interfere with death and what truly belongs to them.</u> **<u>You cannot continue to save death's children because you are not their choice. So truly let these people go because at the end of the day, it's not worth it. You are hurting and I'm hurting. Look at how I hurt for liking the wrong people. We both have to let go of certain things. We're both looking for something</u>**

that humans; some humans cannot give. So instead of seeking, continuing to search in the wrong direction and in the wrong people including spirits; let's find what we need in each other infinitely and indefinitely forever ever without end and live.

Lovey, in all you've done you've prolonged the pain and suffering of your people and this must stop. Death found a way in and look at the planet earth today. Littered with death, violence; all manner of evil; sin.

Evil cannot be reformed so I truly don't know why anyone would think this way. Evil is evil. Evil cannot be good, it can only be evil; negative energy.

Good, evil will always seek to eliminate Good God; hence evil has done all to take humanity from you. Evil give humans what is not his and humans on a whole cannot see this. The offerings of evil is too good to pass up. But what humans and or humanity do not know is there's a cost to what Death and his people have and has given them. And that's the death of their spirit and family. Yes this is sad but it's the reality of billions.

You and I know evil cannot maintain and sustain this earth. Evil feed off negative energy, hence the billions that praise and worship death globally.

Evil sees good as a hindrance, so evil will always seek to destroy and kill all who are good and true to you. You know this; hence I am no exception to the rule. But it must stop because the time of death is over. Give death his true people and let's live come on now.

Forget it; I do not deal in Obeah or Voodoo hence I tell you to let wicked and evil people go. I will not dirty myself for them or to save them. Stop trying to save wicked and evil people. Look at the damage to the soil, people and waterways of earth and tell me if the environment is deserving of it?

Tell me if the universe is deserving of it.
Tell me if you are deserving of it.

And no one dare say this or that because I know the goodness of my mother and grandmother including great grandmother.

I know the goodness of me and you Good God, hence I will never petition You for the wicked and evil again. Hence I've let Jamaica go. You gave them and the black race based on hue and goodness something good and they threw it away for the offerings of

MY MANY QUESTIONS TO GOD

death. Lovey you gave them a name and they tainted it and the land you gave them. So tell me why should anyone pray for us knowing the evils we've done and the ungratefulness of spirit; each and every human?

Female Death is the one to take all when she's pissed off not male death and you know this. I interfered with the Death of Jamaicans more than once and she female death is pissed off at me. Hence I've learnt not to interfere or stand in her way. Jamaica is hers, so let her have her wicked and evil people.

Jamaicans did not want you nor did they choose you, so let them be. Remember dem mek di dutty and stinking Germans burn the Jamaican Flag (your flag of life); suh mek dem suffa because I will never forgive any Jamaican for this. Dem too fucking wutliss. But if dem can sell Air Jamaica (Air God) to the trinity (three dads), father, son and holy ghost (Trinidad) then nothing should surprise me when it comes to them.

Michelle
March 17 and 18, 2015

Lovey I am so angry this morning that I truly don't care if all in humanity hates me because I have no compassion for wicked and evil people including spirits.

Okay here I go because you are truly pissing me off because you are not hearing me and I tired of repeating myself to you.

Lovey, yu hate (8) mi?
Yu truly hate (8) mi?

Don't because my temper is flaring. What the hell part of no wicked and evil people and spirits do you not understand, over stand or comprehend?

I want none in our land and lands, kingdom and abode including homes, business, banks and or financial institutions, schools, hospitals, pharmacies, grocery stores, funeral homes, waterways, seas, oceans, rivers, lakes, streams, ponds, trees, food, body, spirit, earth, the universe and all that I have not mentioned more than permanently, infinitely and indefinitely more than forever ever without end.

I lock out all wicked and evil people and spirits everywhere evil resides especially in the spiritual realm and universe more than forever ever without end.

Lovey you are pissing me off royally with the spiritual evil bullshit.

Lovey I am flying with you now and you are allowing white people, this white woman to steal my plane ticket with you. Now I have to be trying to find it. Mi affi a tek out mi clothes inna public fi people fi si and mi clothes crush up seaka mi affi a look fi mi ticket.

Mi pink car (volts wagon) that belonged to my brother wey mi park dem tow. Yes I parked illegally but still. Lovey yes I saw the beautiful clothes and I wanted to buy some hence I have to go back to LA by truly Lovey, do I have to?

Lovey hear me and listen to me. I do not want to do anything illegal when it comes to you. Nor do I want to do anything illegal for that matter. Hence I've told you before; we need to have our own financial institutions – banks if the banks of man is not for you. I truly do not mind opening up our own bank in the Cayman Islands because this is where you want me to be. I told you, I do not like flat lands and this land is flat but monetary wise I will have your bank and home there. I will not deny you this because I am not about tax evasion. I am not about this bullshit. We are not thieves and I don't intend to live like one or do any dealings like one.

Pay your damned taxes come on now.

Also, my identity is mine and I refuse to allow you to let anyone steal it or use me or our name as a pawn. I refuse this so why the bleep are you allowing them to steal my identity and prosperity with you. What part of impenetrable defences do you not comprehend, over stand and understand? Mi nuh waane nuh evil roune me or come near mi so where does the problem lie? Stop pissing me off man come on now.

The money that I put away in our bank account must go towards helping our land (s) and people. If money is needed for education and heath let it be granted, but under no circumstances must a penny go towards any church including synagogues and mosques or anyone that is wicked and evil. Not even dem pickney. Not one cent should go towards funding bullshit war and wars and the hatred of anyone thereof. I refuse to allow this. I've worked too damned hard, cussed you rude and reckless, was brutal with you for any wicked and evil person or spirit to come share in our prosperity. I refuse this. No evil anywhere including evil spirit can share in our prosperity of goodness, cleanliness, truth and true love; true good will more than infinitely and indefinitely forever ever without end. Never ever let it happen so truly please stop these spiritual demons and physical demons from taking my prosperity health wise and financially. Good God I can't be doing; trying and you are letting these demons condemn me and taking what rightfully belongs to me. Come on it stops right now because you can put a stoppage to this. Hence I tell you to separate Good from Evil everywhere more than indefinitely forever ever and you are not listening to me.

I told you, the children of the seeds you've given me must be good and true, honest and clean and their children's children must be good and true, clean, positive, educated, honest. No evil must any of us come to know. Our genes physical and spiritual DNA must not carry the genes of sin and evil. No wickedness of sin must we know or come to have more than infinitely and indefinitely forever ever without end. This means evil cannot use us as a bye to get in or gain access or entry to our world and worlds, kingdoms and abode ever again. What part of this can't you comprehend on a physical and spiritual level? Mi an sin a nuh fren so why are you pissing me off? Listen come on now. We all need happiness but obviously from the looks of this you don't. You like to see me angry and in pain. Grow up; you have truth and my true desire so where does the problem lie with you?

I've told you, all when dem (we) do not ask you for good pickney, all di pickney dem fi bi good, clean, positive, honest, true, peaceful, truly loving. This also goes for the mates of our choosing. We must all be good and true, clean and honest; positive not just to you but to others; our people, the earth, the universe, the waterways; environment; all that surrounds us.

What the hell do you not get?

I am more than tired of evil taking my wealth and prosperity Good God. I can't deal with evil anymore and I am tired of you letting this happen. I am tired, what do you not get in this?

All must be impenetrable between me and you and our people so no one should come and take a penny from us. No one should come an sey dem a sue us; me. If anyone do this, then don't stop raining down hail bigger than a football or basketball on that person and land. Rain down brimstone of fire on them and their land. I refuse to have anyone cheat me and you and our people including land and lands. This goes for the evil spirits that is doing this bullshit.

I am serious Good God. I've suffered too long to have wicked and evil spirits including humans cheat us.

I've also told you in another book, the money I put away for you and our good and true people including land and lands, no government can say half belongs to me. Truss me when they do this more than hailstorms, fires, thunders, tsunamis will devour them because my fury is worse than these elements combined. Absolutely no one can cheat anyone. I refuse it and you know this but yet you are angering me.

I've also told you, no shirt or skirt, male or female that I am involved with if you let me be involved with anyone or marry anyone, or commit to anyone, not even my children and family, not even death and his people can come and say, Michelle has gone home to Good God; You to rest so I am entitled to half. Absolutely none because these funds cannot be shared with them hence not a penny can none get. This money belongs to the land and lands and good and true people you have and has given me, so truly tell me what the hell I am missing because I truly don't know.

I will however make provisions for my children, family and mate that you have given me. If I have no mate then so be it. I cannot force you to give me something and or someone you cannot.

This money is good and clean hence it must help good and clean people and lands that need it. If they don't need it, let the money stay until it is needed. If houses need to be built to help our good and true people, then let houses be built but not a penny should go towards evil. If anyone use a penny to do evil then all will be taken from that person and land. I refuse the bullshit of wickedness and evil come on now. I refuse to sacrifice what we have for wicked and evil people, wicked and evil spirits and wicked and evil land and lands come on now.

Like I've said, I am different from anyone else; hence I have to help build you in a positive, good and true way. We all say we love but how many truly loves you?

Truly think Lovey because I am tired of the bullshit that is being handed to me by wicked and evil people, wicked and evil spirits including you.

IF YOU CANNOT GIVE GOOD AND TRUE GOOD GOD THEN DON'T GIVE AT ALL.

Don't say you love us so and continue to let wicked and evil spirits and people hurt us. This is not fair and no matter how you think mi stink and rude, I have to say my peace. You are my true love and whether you like it or not, you more than complete me. So truly let me do the good I need to do for you and our people before it's too late. Evil can no longer hinder me come on now. Truly think because I do care and you know this.

I need what's good for you, so stop hindering me from building that which is good and true for us and our good and true people and lands.

Listen Lovey, you know me when it comes to you. I truly do not joke around because time is precious hence you are precious to me.

We can build, so let's build more than solid and impenetrable all around.

I've said my peace, so let's truly live in peace not pieces.

Michelle and Michelle Jean
March 17 and 18, 2015

OTHER BOOKS BY MICHELLE JEAN

Blackman Redemption – The Fall of Michelle Jean
Blackman Redemption – After the Fall Apology
Blackman Redemption – World Cry – Christine Lewis
Blackman Redemption
Blackman Redemption – The Rise and Fall of Jamaica
Blackman Redemption – The War of Israel
Blackman Redemption – The Way I Speak to God
Blackman Redemption – A Little Talk With Man
Blackman Redemption – The Den of Thieves
Blackman Redemption – The Death of Jamaica
Blackman Redemption – Happy Mother's Day
Blackman Redemption – The Death of Faith
Blackman Redemption – The War of Religion
Blackman Redemption – The Death of Russia
Blackman Redemption – The Truth
Blackman Redemption – Spiritual War
Blackman Redemption – The Youths
Blackman Redemption – Black Man Where Is Your God?

The New Book of Life
The New Book of Life – A Cry For The Children
The New Book of Life – Judgement
The New Book of Life – Love Bound
The New Book of Life – Me
The New Book of Life – Life

Just One of Those Days
Book Two – Just One of Those Days
Just One of Those Days – Book Three The Way I Feel
Just One of Those Days – Book Four

MY MANY QUESTIONS TO GOD

The Days I Am Weak
Crazy Thoughts – My Book of Sin
Broken
Ode to Mr. Dean Fraser

A Little Little Talk
A Little Little Talk – Book Two

Prayers
My Collective
A Little Talk/A Time For Fun and Play
Simple Poems
Behind The Scars
Songs of Praise And Love

Love Bound
Love Bound – Book Two

Dedication Unto My Kids
More Talk
Saving America From A Woman's Perspective
My Collective the Other Side of Me
My Collective the Dark Side of Me
A Blessed Day
Lose To Win
My Doubtful Days – Book One

My Little Talk With God
My Little Talk With God – Book Two

A Different Mood and World – Thinking

My Nagging Day
My Nagging Day – Book Two

Friday September 13, 2013
My True Love
It Would Be You
My Day

A Little Advice – Talk
1313, 2032, 2132 – The End of Man
Tata

MICHELLE'S BOOK BLOG – BOOKS 1 – 20

My Problem Day
A Better Way
Stay – Adultery and the Weight of Sin – Cleanliness
Message

Let's Talk
Lonely Days – Foundation
A Little Talk With Jamaica – As Long As I Live
Instructions For Death
My Lonely Thoughts
My Lonely Thoughts – Book Two
My Morning Talks – Prayers With God
What A Mess
My Little Book
A Little Word With You
My First Trip of 2015
Black Mother – Mama Africa
Islamic Thought
My California Trip January 2015
My True Devotion by Michelle – Michelle Jean